Chase One Rabbit:

Strategic Marketing for Business Success

63 Tips, Techniques and Tales for Creative Entrepreneurs

David Parrish

If you chase two rabbits, both will escape.

– Chinese proverb

WORDSCAPES

Chase One Rabbit: Strategic Marketing for Business Success

First published in 2014 by
Wordscapes Ltd
Elevator Studios
27 Parliament Street
Liverpool, L8 5RN
England

www.wordscape.org.uk

ISBN: 978-0-9576945-4-5

A CIP Catalogue record for this book is available from the British Library.

Publisher and Editor-in-Chief: Fiona Shaw
Editor: Gary Smailes
Designer, Typesetter and Producer: Ken Ashcroft
Proofreader: Judith Mansell

Dedication

This book is dedicated to entrepreneurs around the world who are combining their creativity with smart business thinking and using strategic marketing to make their enterprises even more successful.

About this book...

Chase one rabbit is aimed at entrepreneurs who want to use smart marketing to make their businesses even more successful. It's useful for businesses at EVERY stage of development, because marketing is relevant to all enterprises, large and small – from start-ups to mature businesses. It draws greatly from the author's extensive experience and expertise in the successful development of creative and digital enterprises in the UK and worldwide, but its key messages apply to every kind of business and organisation.

This book is designed for busy people, and contains 63 short sections grouped into ten parts. Each short section is useful in itself and is intended to be thought-provoking and practical; each ends with key points and suggestions about what you can do next to put them into action. Reading a section and deciding what to do next will take less than ten minutes. It's a book you can dip into every day and find something to improve the marketing of your business.

Chase one rabbit focuses on the most important aspects of strategic marketing and highlights areas where changes can have the most positive effect. The aim is for you to do the least work for the maximum benefit. It's not a comprehensive textbook of marketing, and doesn't attempt to cover every aspect of this huge subject.

Sections are grouped together, but there are also links to related sections in other parts of the book where relevant. Some people will prefer to hop about within the book; others will read it systematically from start to finish. It's up to you.

The messages about marketing apply to goods, services and projects. However, for brevity and clarity, the term *product* is used throughout to refer to all of these. The points made relate equally well to services and projects, as well as physical products.

The stories in the book are basically true, but sometimes a little poetic licence has been used to elaborate a point, or tell a more memorable tale. In some cases details have been changed so as not to embarrass anybody.

About the author...

David Parrish is a management consultant, trainer and speaker who advises design, media and technology businesses in the creative and digital industries. Based in the UK, David specialises in strategic marketing and has worked in more than 30 countries around the world. Amongst his many other professional accreditations he is a member of the Chartered Institute of Marketing (CIM) in the UK and is a CIM Chartered Marketer.

www.davidparrish.com

Table of Contents

Part Three

Part Four

Part Five

Part Nine

Part Ten

Conclusion

Introduction:
Marketing is not a fancy word for 'selling'

Marketing is vital for any enterprise. But this is not because marketing is about promoting and selling products. Marketing is much more fundamental than that. It's about designing your business with markets in mind. Strategic marketing focuses on choosing the right customers to buy your products, before you start to do any selling.

Strategic marketing is the vital matter of making the right products, selecting the best customers, and then managing the relationship with those selected customers. It's about aligning your whole business to the changing needs of the most important customers.

I wrote my first book, *T-Shirts and Suits: A Guide to the Business of Creativity*[1] to help creative entrepreneurs use a range of business techniques in ways that fit with their own creativity and values, to achieve the success they strive for. I wrote *Chase One Rabbit: Strategic Marketing for Business Success* because, in my experience of helping hundreds of creative businesses around the world, entrepreneurs consistently seek my advice about marketing.

As a consultant, I help creative businesses become even more successful by advising them on the most important aspect of marketing – strategic marketing.

Most people misunderstand what marketing really means. They think it's just a fancy word for selling. Often, what they are talking about is 'selling', but 'marketing' sounds more sophisticated. Hence the first confusion – that marketing really just means 'selling', 'promotion' or 'advertising'. But in fact marketing is much deeper than that. Marketing is a much more comprehensive process of understanding your business, its position amongst competitors and its connection to carefully selected customers. The word 'marketing' is a problem because it means different things to different people.

---

1   www.tss-book.com

Business owners often ask me to help them to improve their businesses. They think that I can help them to sell their product even if the business has much more radical problems. It's as if they think that in my briefcase I have some kind of 'magic dust' that I can sprinkle onto any product to make it miraculously sell more. They think that marketing is just a matter of improving the advertising or publicity associated with their product. So they think that I will solve all their problems with some improved promotional tricks or techniques.

If only it were so simple.

Unfortunately I don't have any 'magic dust', despite what clients want. If only! In fact I **do** help clients using my marketing expertise – but not in the way they first expect. I help them to increase sales and profitability by looking at the business in a much more fundamental way. This involves looking at the whole business from a strategic marketing point of view. I help them to devise effective methods to achieve their business goals. The result is a unique marketing strategy for each business. This book looks at the elements you need to consider in order to devise a unique marketing strategy for your own business.

Underpinning my advice to my clients, and to you in reading this book, is my approach to marketing, which makes a clear distinction between strategic marketing and operational marketing (operational marketing is also sometimes called marketing communications or 'marketing comms'). This difference is crucial. And it is the mistake of not differentiating between these two aspects of marketing that causes so many problems in the first place.

This book explains why a strategic approach to marketing results in success. It's full of real stories about entrepreneurs who have used smart strategic marketing. Many of these stories are about my own clients and some are from my own experience. The book offers a range of insights that can be applied directly to your own business. And it suggests practical things you can do immediately to make your enterprise even more successful.

Part One begins with a true story about a furniture maker
called Nick and how he used strategic thinking to devise his
authentic marketing...

First things first
Thinking strategically about marketing

Strategic marketing must come first. Strategic marketing is about the 'big picture'. Before starting to sell, we need to decide which are the right customers to sell to. Only then do we consider our marketing messages and the media to use.

Many failures of business that are blamed on 'marketing' are actually more fundamental failures of strategic marketing, not mistakes of operational marketing. Usually, the people at the top make these strategic marketing errors, not the 'marketing department'.

Marketing communications can be creative and eye-catching, but also part of a carefully designed marketing strategy. By using both artistic creativity and a broader ingenuity, we can be smart about marketing and make our enterprises even more successful.

1 Authentic marketing

Nick was an expert furniture maker. His products were more than furniture – they were works of art. Clearly, his products were not for everybody, but for those people who appreciated his craftsmanship and creativity, they were a delight.

Nick was an introvert and told me that he 'couldn't do marketing'. He was becoming stressed because he needed more customers, but found that direct selling was extremely uncomfortable for him. He was not a natural 'salesman' and felt out of place at business networking events. He was embarrassed that his website was not as well designed as it might be, especially because friends kept telling him that he needed a better one. Other friends and associates told him he should use social media more, especially Facebook and Twitter, because these were popular and effective.

Nick felt that marketing wasn't his strength and he needed help to sell his creations, so he engaged a marketing consultant.

This consultant suggested he rent a shop in the high street. When it turned out that sales were below the levels needed to pay the rent and other costs, the consultant suggested that Nick improve his selling skills by going on a sales training course. He also suggested redesigning his website and using search engine optimisation to improve his Google ranking for furniture searches. He also suggested increased use of social media, and advertising in the local newspaper to drive more traffic to his high street store.

Nick found himself spending a lot of money and time on these things. He was exhausted much of the time, but, despite doing as advised, these techniques didn't generate the sales that the consultant had forecast. Then the consultant said that the problem was that Nick's prices were too high for the local market. So he advised Nick to make cheaper furniture, to be sold at a lower price. Of course, that meant he'd have to sell more items to make the same profit...

None of this felt right to Nick.

Even though he admitted he wasn't a marketing expert, Nick began to have doubts about the consultant's advice. Despite paying substantial consultancy fees, sales were flat and Nick was running out of money fast. It just wasn't working. He sacked the consultant.

By now Nick was disillusioned with marketing and in despair about his business. In his mind, 'marketing' meant the painful process of trying to sell to somebody who simply wasn't interested. After his encounter with the consultant he concluded that 'marketing' meant a bag of tricks, gimmicks and techniques to get people who don't want your stuff to buy it. None of the advice he had received about these techniques felt right to him. And anyway, none of it had worked. Everything about 'marketing' was alien to him.

Nick was at his wit's end when he turned to me for business advice.

The first thing I did was sit down and ask questions about his business, including about the customers he had sold to so far, and how he had found them. He told me that it was usually by word-of-mouth. For example, he said that the previous weekend he had visited a married couple, who had bought some of his furniture and subsequently become friends. He had called in on them for a cup of coffee and a chat. By coincidence, they had visitors with them for a few days, some friends from another part of the country. These friends of his friends were interested in his work and very much appreciated his creativity. They asked him about his inspiration, the materials he used, his techniques, and his workshop. Nick responded enthusiastically, telling them about every aspect of his creative endeavours. He was in his element. He wasn't 'marketing'; he wasn't trying to sell anything. He was merely talking about his passion to people who were 'on the same wavelength'. By the time he had left the house the visiting couple had commissioned him to make two pieces of furniture for them. They were expensive items but they paid 50% upfront. I smiled wryly when he told me he was 'no good at marketing'.

Actually, he communicates brilliantly, authentically and enthusiastically when connected with the *right* customers, so much so that he doesn't feel he is selling at all.

As a result of my conversation with Nick, my marketing advice was very different from that of the previous consultant.

Nick's fundamental problem was that in his high street shop he was trying to sell to the wrong kind of customers. Most people want to buy inexpensive functional furniture, not expensive works of art. The problem was not a lack of sales skills, or the absence of advertising or the under-use of social media. None of these things work if you are using them to try to sell to the wrong kind of customer. The first consultant didn't consider selecting the right customers, so he was part of the problem, not part of the solution.

If the strategy – that is, the focus on the correct type of customer – is wrong, then it will make no difference what techniques are employed. Identifying the correct customer is always the first step.

The first marketing consultant was focusing only on operational marketing, or marketing communications, not at all on marketing strategy. He was looking at techniques, not asking the wider question, 'who will buy this furniture?' He was trying to use (operational) marketing techniques to sell to the wrong kind of customers. Smart marketing is about selecting the right kind of customers first. I focus on strategic marketing first, only later on marketing communications.

As a strategic marketing consultant, my approach would **not** be to send him on a sales training course, so that he could sell to uninterested people. I would **not** advise him to try to sell to the general public in the high street. Neither would I suggest he advertises in the local newspaper to attract customers to his shop. I certainly would **not** advise him to drop his prices to fit the expectations of the general public.

My task was to work with Nick to devise a marketing strategy that worked for his business. My job was to help him use marketing in a way that was consistent with his objectives and values.

Our strategy involved identifying the correct market for his products – identifying the type of person who would be excited to buy his furniture. The strategy was to put Nick in front of the right kind of potential customers and allow him to be his authentic self.

Selling should not be painful. If selling is difficult, then perhaps that's an indication that we're dealing with the wrong kind of customers. In contrast, when we are connected to the right kind of customers, marketing communication is easy. If we get the strategy right, selling becomes superfluous.

Using his marketing strategy Nick found people who shared his values and enthusiasm. This strategy wasn't only about Nick's personal style, his creative passion and his business values. It was also the correct formula for appropriate, cost-effective, and successful marketing. It was his formula for business success.

For Nick, it is important that he is his authentic self. This is not just good for Nick; it's good for his business. We should be true to ourselves, honest with customers, and in harmony with our values and passions. These are not just nice bonuses to attach to our business lives; they are part and parcel of being a successful entrepreneur. I wanted to ensure people were not buying just great furniture, but great furniture made by Nick. He was part of the product.

Nick used my strategic marketing advice to realign his creative products with the right kind of customers – he decided not to try to sell to the general public on the high street and closed his shop. He followed word of mouth recommendations and found that he had a small number of highly profitable 'super fans' who bought his furniture from him at full price, again and again. He now works only with customers who are in harmony with his creativity, values and pricing. Nick is a successful creative entrepreneur.

This true story of the two consultants illustrates nicely two very different approaches to marketing.

The first is to use a 'bag of tricks' to try and sell to the wrong kind of customers; the second is about finding the right kind of customers, who fit with your business and don't need to be 'sold to'. The first adviser was a consultant in marketing communications; the second a consultant in strategic marketing.

Decide for yourself which kind of marketing can best help you to become even more successful.

Key Points

Being authentic in business means being yourself and being 'in your element'. Strategic marketing is about finding customers who are on your wavelength – then selling to them is easy and natural, not a painful process.

What to do next

• Review past and current customers and identify the ones with whom you are on the same wavelength. With which customers and in which situations are you 'in your element'? Use this approach as a compass to find the right kind of customers.

• Write down, in priority order, customers you are most in tune with. Identify their key characteristics to help identify more customers of the same type.

See also...

2 Marketing makes selling superfluous

The beauty of strategic marketing is that if you get it right, you don't need to do the 'hard sell'. In fact, if your strategic marketing is right, there's much less need for operational marketing. As Peter Drucker famously said, 'The purpose of marketing is to make selling superfluous'.

Strategic marketing is not something that can be added on at the end. It must permeate the whole business, from start to finish, from top to bottom. Strategic marketing is about designing and developing a business with customers in mind at all times. It is not a separate function; it is a fundamental business philosophy.

In contrast, for people who think the word marketing merely means 'selling', marketing activity comes last. This is often the case in unsuccessful businesses. They make a product without thinking about the market and then they end up with the problem of selling it. They engage sales people and adopt expensive advertising techniques. They build a whole new 'marketing department' to try and sell products. In other words, they see marketing as a bolt on to the business.

The strategic marketing approach I advocate takes a different view. It's a philosophy that marketing is about aligning the whole business around the changing needs of selected customers. This is what David Packard meant in his well-known quote, 'Marketing is too important to be left to the marketing department.'

If I could offer businesses just one piece of marketing advice it would be this: deal with strategic marketing issues first. It's only when the business is correctly designed around the needs of selected customers that we should consider operational marketing techniques.

Key Points

Strategic marketing is about the business as a whole and its design
and development around the changing needs of selected customers.
It is not a separate department or final stage in the process.

What to do next

• Focus on the strategic marketing of your business. Have you
  designed your products around the needs of selected customers?
  Realign strategic marketing if necessary before looking at
  marketing communications.

• List the customers to whom you don't have to do the 'hard sell'.
  Conversely, list the customers on whom you are expending
  selling energy without success.

See also...

3 Strategy is invisible

One of the reasons that strategic marketing is overlooked is because it's not obvious; it's not 'in our faces'. Strategy is practically invisible to outsiders, because it is the thinking behind the scenes within businesses that we never get to see.

What we **do** see, as consumers and observers of businesses, is the advertising, social media, promotional activities, public relations and other visible techniques that are the result of marketing communications work. We see the end result that is delivered to us as TV adverts, websites, apps, and messages in many other media.

What we don't see is the clear-headed strategic thinking that has gone on behind the scenes, months earlier. This strategic thinking involves deciding on particular market segments to target, exact messages, and the most appropriate media to deliver those messages.

Consequently we are unaware of the decisions made in boardrooms and offices about which particular operational marketing techniques to use – and which **not** to use.

We don't hear about the decision **not** to advertise to a particular market segment. We never see the advertisements that businesses choose **not** to run. Nobody tells us about the decisions **not** to use a particular medium to get a message to a chosen target market.

The casual observer may conclude that advertisers use every opportunity to promote all products to as many people as possible, but it isn't so.

Sometimes we see advertising which is unusual, avant-garde, amusing or even apparently silly, and there's a danger that we see marketing people as purely zany creatives, having fun, simply seeking attention, and then calling it 'creative marketing'.

Because we can be enchanted, amused and fascinated by advertising glitz and glamour, this is the aspect of marketing that we tend to focus on. Indeed we are often inspired and want to copy those techniques. But mass marketing techniques, even when scaled down, are not appropriate to smaller businesses.

Don't focus only on the visible aspects of marketing; think also about the strategy behind them.

Key Points

Marketing starts in the boardroom, not on the billboard.

Some of the most important marketing decisions are strategic ones about what **not** to do. Strategic marketers decide which people **not** to target and which media **not** to use.

What to do next

- Make sure that decisions about what media to use are based on strategy, not the result of an enchantment with a particular medium.

- Make it a rule for yourself and your colleagues that you will only decide which media to use after considering their relevance to specific messages to be delivered to particular market segments.

See also...

4 How not to sell food to the French

On the UK TV show *The Apprentice*, Sir Alan Sugar once challenged the teams of would-be apprentices to go to France to sell food on the market in a small town in Normandy. One team did particularly badly: not only did they make less profit than their rival teams, but they actually lost money. The leader and his team were called in to Sir Alan's boardroom to account for their actions. As I watched I could feel my blood pressure rising. The leader defended himself by saying that it was a failure of marketing and tried to blame his colleague, who was responsible for the advertising banners, leaflets and other promotional materials.

In fact the leader was half right: it was a marketing problem, but not the marketing problem he identified.

By the word 'marketing' he meant 'operational marketing' and he was trying to blame the person responsible for advertising and promotion. The real failure was a marketing mistake made by the team leader himself – a gross mistake of strategic marketing.

Before going off to France, the leader decided to sell cheese to the French. He went to a wholesaler and bought a large block of factory-produced cheese, wrapped in plastic, to sell on the French market. Generally speaking, the French have little respect for English food. Moreover, the French love food and are discerning about cheese, especially in Normandy. There is no way that the good people of Normandy will buy factory-produced English cheese. Not even if it is presented on cute cocktail sticks. Not even if it were backed up by millions of euros worth of TV advertising. **This** was the marketing problem – made by the leader himself – which meant that their business was fundamentally flawed. It was not the fault of the person producing the promotional materials. It was nothing to do with operational marketing and everything to do with strategic marketing.

As an epilogue to the story, other teams were relatively successful. They thought about the market and tried to think of the few English food products that the French might actually buy. The more successful teams were those that chose to sell marmalades, pickles, and chutneys.

Many of the biggest problems in business can be ascribed to mistakes in strategic marketing. Don't blame the operational marketing people if your product doesn't sell. Instead you may need to look towards the people who make strategic marketing errors (even if they don't call what they do 'marketing').

Strategic marketing means connecting the right products to the right customers.

Key Points

Many failures of business that are blamed on marketing (operational marketing) are actually more fundamental failures of strategic marketing. The people at the top, not the 'marketing department', make those strategic marketing errors.

What to do next

- Instead of blaming failures of operational marketing for lack of sales, consider the possibility that the marketing **strategy** is wrong. Don't blame the 'marketing department' for mistakes that are the responsibility of the key decision makers.

- Give the sales department the opportunity to speak out if they believe they are being asked to achieve unreasonable targets as a result of misjudgements in strategic marketing. Better still, involve the sales department at an early stage, when deciding what to produce because they are closest to customers and more likely to understand their needs.

See also...

20 Not all customers are good customers!   *60*

5 Is there a market in the gap?

Many years ago, as a young man, I set up a bookshop in my small home town near Manchester, England with some friends. The bookshop was never as commercially successful as we'd hoped. With hindsight, the reason for the failure was that our small town, so close to a big city, was not in the right position to support its own bookshop at that time. Years later, I learnt that big businesses undertake a demographic analysis in order to choose sites for their retail operations. They carefully assess which locations and communities have the right number and type of customers to produce the profits they require.

We didn't evaluate the size of the market objectively; we just looked around our town, saw no bookshop and decided to open one. The market was not quite right for our product at that time. In setting up the first bookshop in the town we thought we had found a gap in the market.

What we should have asked is the question: *is there a market in the gap?* Or more precisely, *is there a big enough market to achieve the sales we need?*

We were focused more on our own enthusiasm to sell books, rather than the size of the market and customers' needs and habits. Because of this, our business was fundamentally flawed.

The strategic marketing problem was that there weren't enough customers in the town to support their own bookshop and many book buyers were still in the habit of travelling into Manchester to buy their books.

Frustrated, we tried all kinds of operational marketing techniques to sell more books, but we were swimming against the tide. We distributed leaflets, advertised in the local newspaper, and we gave away bookmarks. But none of these efforts fixed the fundamental problem. This is another example of strategic marketing trumping operational marketing. Get the fundamentals right and operational marketing is relatively easy. Make a mistake of strategic marketing and you will always be on the back foot.

As a footnote, although the bookshop was never as commercially successful as we had hoped, I have absolutely no regrets. For one, our definition of success was not entirely about making money. It was a cultural project to make books available, and a community enterprise involved in spreading the word and empowering people. Secondly, I learnt a tremendous amount about business in that enterprise, through the mistakes we made, and the successes we achieved. I learnt about cash flow, contracts, taxation, accountancy and managing people. I learnt about the importance of strategic marketing over operational marketing. The experience made me hungry to learn more about business, which I did over many subsequent years. I continued to learn from managing more commercially successful enterprises, from business school and from my consultancy clients. In the long run, the bookshop experience made me a better entrepreneur.

Key Points

Strategic marketing is about the 'big picture' questions:

- Is there a sufficiently large market for your product?
- **Why** aren't competitors serving a market?
- What are the habits and preferences of your target customers?

What to do next

- Don't let your heart rule your head. Objectively assess market opportunities. Examine which markets your competitors are serving – and which ones they aren't selling to. Why aren't they? Do they know something we don't? Is there a viable market?
- Test the market with a controlled pilot project or real feasibility study.

- Insist that you select market segments only after you have explained their viability in writing by yourself or a relevant colleague.

See also...

6 The big fight: sales vs. production

I had the privilege of being invited to lecture in strategic marketing at a business school in Shanghai, China. I spent six months in the country and it was fascinating to watch the struggle between the academics and the business development department. The academics said that the business development department should go out and sell the courses the academics had devised. The business development department argued that the academics should create courses that potential customers actually wanted. The academics blamed poor sales effort and 'marketing' techniques for the lack of sales of their courses. The business development people blamed the academics for not being focused on customers' needs, just their own academic interests.

Although I wasn't directly involved in this battle, it was fascinating to watch. It was also enlightening because I had seen the same fight in other contexts. I've seen similar conflicts in businesses, charities and voluntary groups in different countries. A charity I advised in England raised money from donors by promising things that couldn't be delivered by other departments. Many commercial enterprises are plagued by a conflict between the sales people and their production departments. In these cases there is always a disconnection between the internal producers and the customer-facing staff. The tensions reveal the cracks below the surface of the business. These are the fault-lines that can result in earthquakes.

As a consultant I have seen many tensions within businesses – indeed outright conflict – between different departments in an enterprise. The 'marketing department' (often just a fancy title for the sales team) is often at odds with those responsible for producing the goods or services at the heart of the business.

One source of conflict is when the sales department is motivated only to achieve sales – at any cost. This results in conflict with the production department, which is left to pick up the pieces after the sales people have promised low prices and quick delivery, making impossible promises but nevertheless earning their bonuses. (By the way, I don't blame the salespeople: I blame the management. Management is responsible for harmoniously aligning the different departments of the business.)

Another source of conflict is the other way around, when the sales department is blamed for lack of sales, when in fact the problem is that the product is not required, or simply not good enough. Or top management is focusing on the wrong target market. Again, I blame the management, who sometimes seem to take the view that anything can be sold if only the 'marketing department' works its magic.

Who's right and who's wrong?

In my view, such battles are the result of a failure of top management. Because it is the people at the top making strategic decisions that need to square the circle. Business strategy is all about harmonising what can feasibly be produced profitably and the exact markets to be served. This involves leadership and tough decisions about which products **not** to produce and which markets **not** to serve. Failure to devise a realistic strategy based on market needs and internal capability produces these conflicts. It creates inefficiency and wastes resources, as well as causing tension and dissatisfaction for employees.

This is essentially a problem of strategic marketing, not operational marketing. And who's responsible for strategic marketing? Not the 'marketing department' but the Chief Executive Officer.

Key Points

Tensions and conflicts between the internal producers and the customer-facing salespeople happen in many businesses and organisations. The underlying reason is a lack of a strategy that harmoniously connects products and markets. This is the responsibility of the top management, even though the people who usually take the flak are at lower levels in the organisation.

What to do next

- Create harmony between departments in your business by devising a clear marketing strategy. This involves deciding which products not to produce and which markets not to serve. Align the interests and incentives of producers and salespeople. This may involve restructuring the organisation and changing responsibilities.

- Ensure that the sales department and the production department speak directly with each other. Any conflicts arising from this must be dealt with by top management.

See also...

7 Quirky but strategic

Cheeky Guerrillas in Utrecht[2] is an article I wrote about a company of graphic designers who ran a guerrilla marketing campaign. Using ladders, they posted large notices onto the outside of office block windows promoting their company and asking the business inside to contact them. In marketing terms, it was outrageous and daring and caught the attention not only of the target clients, but the business community as a whole.

What were they doing? Was it legal? Were they mad?

Though the activity was spectacular, what was not immediately evident was the strategic thinking behind it. Before climbing ladders with posters and paste brushes, the partners in the business had spent a lot of time carefully analysing the market for their work.

- They took the time to understand competitors in order to identify their firm's competitive advantage

- They carefully prioritised target customers in order to decide which were the most important few they should contact in this way

It wasn't a crazy idea at all; indeed it was rigorous strategic thinking, undertaken soberly in the company's boardroom. The point is, this was a serious marketing campaign based on sound marketing strategy, not just some random theatrical stunt.

Another example of how marketing can be 'quirky but strategic' is a marketing campaign undertaken by a small advertising agency called Peppered Sprout featured in my earlier book *T-Shirts and Suits: A Guide to the Business of Creativity*[3]. Unlike many of their rivals, who accepted all kinds of small projects in the early years of their business, Peppered Sprout was ambitious from the start. Taking inspiration from David Ogilvy and his story told in the book *Confessions of an Advertising Man*, Peppered Sprout drew up a hit

---

2 www.tss-ideasinaction.com

3 www.tss-book.com

list of potential clients. One of these was footwear manufacturer Puma UK. This was an ambitious target client for such a small and new advertising agency. The owners knew this and understood that they would have to do something special to grab the attention of this potential client. In many ways, this was their biggest problem. They were confident that if they had the chance to actually speak to one of the top executives within Puma UK, they would be able to win a contract for one of Puma's advertising campaigns.

But how could they get past the gatekeepers? Clearly, emails would not be effective and even a written letter was likely to generate a polite rejection, or end up in the waste paper bin.

Having decided strategically and logically about their objectives, they switched from left-brain thinking to right-brain thinking and conjured up some imaginative ideas. As a result, what they did was this: They took a Puma sports shoe and cut it along its seams, so that it opened up and could be placed on a woman's head like some kind of surreal headgear. They engaged a model and a fashion photographer to take a photo of the Puma shoe, worn in this way. Then they featured the photograph on the front of their in-house magazine. Then they sent a copy of this magazine by courier, with a covering letter, to the Managing Director of Puma UK. Within 24 hours, they'd received a personal phone call from the MD, inviting them to a meeting. By using their creativity to make such an impact, they were able to reach the decision maker. As a result of the meeting that followed, they were commissioned to create an advertising campaign for one of Puma's products.

I congratulate the entrepreneurs behind these examples of creative marketing. In both cases they combined clear strategic thinking in the boardroom together with imaginative and eye-catching action. In this way, marketing can be both strategic and quirky.

Key Points

Marketing communications are often very creative, even quirky. But this doesn't mean that they're illogical. There is often a method in the madness. Marketing communications can be quirky, but also part of a well thought through marketing strategy.

What to do next

• Create a strategic marketing framework before brainstorming to find imaginative, creative and quirky ways to communicate key messages to target markets.

See also...

8 a-Creativity: i-Creativity

Marketing can be both strategic **and** quirky, using two different kinds of creativity.

We have a problem with the word 'creativity'. In the English language, the word creativity usually implies some kind of **artistic** creativity. As a consequence, many people have told me that they're 'not creative', by which they mean that they are not artistically gifted. However, these same people are wonderfully creative in terms of building their businesses, developing new products, inspiring people, forming partnerships, and managing complex enterprises.

I suggest that we should have two definitions for the word creativity. I first proposed this idea in a keynote speech at TEDx Napoli[4]. I coined two new terms: firstly 'a-Creativity' when we mean artistic creativity; and 'i-Creativity' to signify a much wider kind of creativity. i-Creativity can also be called 'ingenuity', 'thinking differently', 'innovation', or simply 'problem-solving'.

In my work with creative entrepreneurs around the world, I'm often stunned by the creativity these talented people exhibit in their work. In their studios they design products, make films, produce music, create computer games or publish books. At the same time, I am often saddened that they don't use their creative capacity equally well in the office. I believe strongly that creativity has a place, not only in the artistic realm, but also in the strategies and techniques of doing business.

Creative people in business can use a-Creativity in the studio and i-Creativity in the business office. Creativity is not exclusively the monopoly of the artist, or something that belongs in the studio. Creativity is an approach to doing things differently in terms of business. Thinking in this way, all sorts of new possibilities open up. For example two art galleries in Ho Chi Minh City in Vietnam decided not to compete directly but to adopt a strategy of

---

4 http://blog.davidparrish.com/tshirts_and_suits/2012/04/a-creativity-i-creativity.html

'co-opetition' to collaborate online[5]. Another example of complementing a-Creativity in the studio with i-Creativity in the office is Brazilian commercial illustrator Guilherme Marconi, who doesn't sell his illustrations but licenses them to major corporations. The article about this is entitled *Don't sell it; rent it*[6]. My free *Ideas in Action* articles online[7] feature creative entrepreneurs using i-Creativity to devise smart business methods.

In terms of marketing, we need to use both a-Creativity and i-Creativity. That's to say, we need to use all our creative capacity both in the office and the studio. We need to make sure that we have the right strategic framework first, before moving on to colourful communications.

Key Points

Marketing can involve using two kinds of creativity: artistic creativity and a more general kind of creativity that is about ingenuity and problem-solving. Let's distinguish the two by calling them a-Creativity and i-Creativity respectively. We can use both kinds of creativity in managing creative enterprises.

What to do next

• Use the terms a-Creativity and i-Creativity to distinguish between the two kinds of creativity. Decide how best each can be used in the studio and the business office.

See also...

---

5 www.tss-ideasinaction.com

6 www.tss-ideasinaction.com

7 www.tss-ideasinaction.com

Now it's time to sit back and reflect on your marketing. Not by looking at sales techniques but by going deeper into the very heart of your business.

Ask yourself about your passions, which customers are your soul mates and what you are going to decide positively *not* to do.

This kind of marketing thinking will help you make your business more authentic, integrated and truly successful.

We also need to be aware of competitors...

PART TWO

Marketing focus
Find your niche amongst competitors

It's better to do one or two things really well than to spread your efforts too thinly, because in most cases customers want a specialist, not a generalist. By offering a wide range of services, you're competing on many different fronts, creating rivals everywhere. Choosing which few things to do involves some hard thinking, which is why most people avoid it. They rush around doing trivial stuff to make sure they have no time to think about strategic issues.

Your business doesn't have any weaknesses, except when you put it in the wrong situation. By being clever, you can connect the characteristics of your business to the right customers and projects, where these characteristics become strengths.

It's not what you are good at that matters; it's the thing you excel at **in relation to rivals** that gives you a competitive advantage. The customers who want your excellence are your ideal customers.

9 Chase one rabbit

A Chinese proverb says, 'if you chase two rabbits, both will escape.' It's best to do one thing really, really well and that's one of the *Ten things that Google has found to be true*. It seems to me that both of these are saying the same thing – one from the East, one from the West; one ancient, one modern.

In a business context my advice to entrepreneurs is often about focusing. Don't try to do too much, but instead do a few things – or even just one thing – really well.

In contrast, what I see too often are businesses that are trying to do too much, spreading their resources too thinly, and consequently being unable to compete effectively with rivals who focus on one particular product. There is a danger of being a 'jack of all trades and master of none'. I see this especially in early-stage businesses that have not yet found their competitive advantage and are offering to do everything.

Miguel attended one of my workshops in Bilbao, Spain. He was a graphic designer who offered a range of services including logo design, stationery sets, signage, leaflets design and print management, rebranding projects, and specialist graphic design such as book layouts. His logic was that the more he offered, the more chance he had of winning new customers. 'If I spread my net widely', he told me, 'I will catch more fish.' On the Internet this translates into more keywords and more potential hits from customers searching for any of these services.

There was only one problem with this plan: customers.

Customers don't always behave in the way that we want them to, and perceive things differently than we do. From a customer's point of view the 'jack of all trades' is indeed a master of none. Miguel increased the number of hits to his website but few of them converted into customers. When visitors arrived at his website, they saw that he was 'jack of all trades', not a specialist in the one keyword that had attracted them to his site in the first place.

Customers don't want somebody who dabbles in all sorts of things; they would rather have an expert, who does exactly what they want.

There's often a mismatch between the way we expect or want customers to behave, and the way we behave ourselves when we are consumers. If you wanted to find an electrician to fix the wiring in your office or home, would you choose one who also offers joinery, plumbing, building, and plastering? Such a multi-talented tradesperson could argue that by advertising all these services they will get more work. I don't think so. I certainly wouldn't want such a generalist to do a specialist's work for me. If customers want an electrician they will engage somebody who is a specialist, somebody who focuses entirely on electrics, and who is an expert in that trade.

Look at your marketing communications from the customers' point of view. Do they want a generalist or a specialist? Why should they buy from you when somebody else specialises in the exact thing they require?

How can you specialise and be the go-to supplier?

Key Points

Customers want a specialist, not a generalist or 'jack of all trades'. It's better to do one or two things really well than to spread your efforts too thinly, only for customers to pass you by on their way to a specialist.

What to do next

- Ask yourself: with what can we specialise and be the go-to supplier? Instead of being a jack of all trades, select a speciality in which we can become a master.

- Decide what you can excel at in relation to the competition. Then promote this excellence to the customers who truly value it.

See also...

18 Positive strategy involves deciding what not to do   *51*

10 Are you a 'busy fool'?

We avoid doing difficult things by occupying ourselves with trivial things. We deal with urgent trivia instead of what's really important. Keeping busy like this allows us to avoid having to make important decisions.

In my work, amongst hundreds of businesses, I see too many people acting like 'busy fools'. These are people who would much rather get busy doing all kinds of promotional activity rather than stop and think. Because thinking hurts. Thinking is the difficult option. Being too busy to think is a get-out, an excuse: it's the easy option. In this way, being busy can be a form of laziness. I agree with Timothy Ferriss who says this in his book *The Four Hour Work Week*.

Working hard can be a diversion from working smart. Being busy with operational marketing activities is easier than thinking hard about the much more important and difficult matters of marketing strategy.

Don't be enchanted by marketing communications and sexy media. Stop frantic promotion to the wrong kind of customers and resist the urge to scatter emails and tweets in all directions. Calm down and think clearly.

Remember that the most important aspect of marketing is about strategy and this is at the heart of the business. Let's differentiate clearly between strategic marketing and operational marketing. Let's make sure that we sort out our strategic marketing first, before dealing with operational marketing matters.

Don't be a busy fool. Slow down and think; work smart, not hard. Be smart about marketing. Think strategic marketing first.

Key Points

It's easier to rush around doing trivial stuff and avoid doing the hard work of thinking about strategic issues. In this way, being busy is a form of laziness.

What to do next

- Stop rushing around. Face up to the hard work of thinking about your marketing strategically. Slow down and think.

- Allocate a specific time for thinking through your marketing strategy, with colleagues or advisers, as appropriate.

See also...

11 How to turn weaknesses into strengths

Margit is the Danish owner of a public relations business. She was frustrated that it was difficult for her small company to win work with large corporations. Although she tendered for contracts and made other approaches, she always seemed to lose out to larger rivals. The relatively small size of her company was a weakness in bidding for work from these clients and so she asked me about how she could address this weakness by growing her company.

We started with an analysis of her company and its markets. Being a relatively small company, it had low fixed costs and was more agile than its larger rivals, with a very good portfolio of smaller clients. Working with these clients on small projects was profitable for Margit's company, whereas larger rivals with higher fixed costs could not service these jobs profitably. In other words, the small size of her company was a strength in terms of delivering smaller projects profitably. We concluded that the most effective strategy was not to win the business of large clients at all, but instead to focus on an area in which her company had competitive advantage – smaller contracts from smaller clients.

Margit could deliver services to small clients profitably – her company didn't need to tender formally, because of the low value of these projects, and she was able to win projects through personal contacts. It was actually more profitable for her small PR company to undertake a large number of smaller contracts, which were easier to win and deliver, than to go through the laborious process of competing with larger rivals in tendering for contracts, and failing more often than not. She decided not to grow the size of the business, but to use the small size of her company where it was a strength. What she did grow were the profits.

The classic 'SWOT' analysis business technique invites you as an entrepreneur to examine the internal **Strengths** and **Weaknesses** of your business, then evaluate the external **Opportunities** and **Threats** relevant to it.

My experience of using SWOT analysis is that working groups report back with lists of features that are both strengths **and** weaknesses (depending on circumstances).

The problem with this approach is that strengths and weaknesses only have meaning within any particular context. A business characteristic can be a strength in one situation, yet the same characteristic could be a weakness in a different arena. For example, an aggressive negotiating style could be a strength in the USA but a weakness in China. A large business might achieve economies of scale but be perceived as impersonal by some customers. A business run by young people might be better able to achieve a rapport with younger customers than with older clients. A company may be regarded as 'exotic' overseas yet quite ordinary in its own country.

So, instead of labelling various facts about a business as either a strength or a weakness, I prefer the more neutral term 'characteristic'. Then, the objective of business strategy is to manoeuvre those characteristics into places within the market where they become strengths.

Business strategy is about making our characteristics become strengths by choosing the right customers and projects. A fact about our business is only a weakness when it's a bad fit with particular clients and projects. Avoid these bad fits and weaknesses disappear. Choose good fits instead and characteristics become strengths.

Be clear about what you are, your values and passions, and in what circumstances you are 'in your element'. Apply the characteristics of yourself and your business in circumstances where they become strengths. Be your authentic self and allow your business to be authentic. Be proud of what you are; be distinctive. Don't try to be like everyone else. As an artist friend of mine says, 'your difference is your strength'. Tell your story: in this way you'll alienate some people, but attract others. Being upfront and open about what you are and what you believe in will polarise the market, from your point of view, into good and bad customers.

Be prepared to say NO to customers that don't fit with your strengths, values and objectives.

Connecting your authentic business with the right kind of customers – that's what marketing is really about. Strategic marketing. Successful marketing. This is how to be successful in business.

Key Points

A business's strengths or weaknesses can only be evaluated in the context of any particular situation – don't change your business, change your situation. Connect the realities of your business to customers and projects where they become strengths.

What to do next

- Search for customers and projects that fit with the characteristics of your business in such a way that so-called weaknesses become strengths.

- Make a list of target customers you can serve better than competitors can.

See also...

12 What's your competitive advantage?

Felipe manages a small video production company in Bogotá, Colombia. When I asked him what his business excels at, he quickly said, 'music videos' and told me about the excellent videos they'd produced for rock bands. He told me they also make corporate videos and videos for community groups with subtitles used for speakers of foreign languages.

My next question was to ask Felipe what could they do well that rivals couldn't. We soon recognised that hundreds of other companies also produce excellent music videos, so his company can't dominate that market. However, very few rivals can produce community-based documentary videos with more than one language involved. In fact, it turned out they are one of the few best firms making multilingual documentaries. Although they excel at music videos, they don't stand out from the crowd in this market. They do not excel **in relation to the competition**. Where they do excel in relation to rivals is in the multilingual documentary business. This is where they have competitive advantage.

At what can you excel? Or more precisely, at what can you excel **in relation to competitors**?

It makes perfect sense to focus on the areas in which you have competitive advantage – to do only those things at which you can excel in relation to competitors. In this way you are competing on your own terms, choosing your battles, and dealing with rivals from a position of strength.

This competitive advantage may be technical, for example, expertise in a particular business area that others do not have. On the other hand, competitive advantage may derive from infrastructure, systems, logistics, or economies of scale that cannot be replicated easily by rivals. For example, wide distribution networks, detailed information about sales trends, production capacity or rapid delivery can provide a competitive advantage over rivals for particular businesses.

Your competitive advantage may be also derived from social connections or status. It may be that you are well respected in a particular community, or have connections in all the right places in a certain industry, or can relate better than rivals to a particular group of customers because of cultural, language, or other affiliations. This is especially the case in businesses where personal relationships matter.

The majority of businesses managed by creative people and selling products derived from that creativity depend on personal relationships. The more closely the customer is involved with the business owners, the more important these personal relationships become. This social advantage doesn't matter in businesses that are purely impersonal.

In other words, it's unimportant when transactions and business can take place without needing to interact with other people, and without it being in the slightest bit important that you know, like, or trust them. The more the customer needs to know, like and trust you, the more we need to emphasise people and the 'personality' of the business in our marketing strategy and communications.

We cannot recognise where we have competitive advantage unless we analyse our competitors.

This is crucial because we need to base our marketing strategy on our competitive advantage. That's to say, if we want to focus on the things we can do better than our rivals, we need to know what our rivals are good at, not so good at, and how we can outmanoeuvre them.

'Know your enemy' is a fundamental principle of warfare and similarly in business we need to know who we're up against, which fights we'll never win, and which battles we **can** win. Jack Welch, CEO of the General Electric Company, talked about how you have to be paranoid to survive. I'm not advocating paranoia but it is in our interest as business people to be aware of our competitors' movements, their strengths and their relative weaknesses, so that we can find the best ways in which we can compete amongst them in a crowded marketplace. Market research can also include finding out about competitors' relative strengths and weaknesses as well as customers' needs.

So, competitive advantage can be based on expertise, business structure or social connections. This is the key to dominating a market. When you dominate a market it changes the power balance between you and your customers, which then affects the price you can charge.

If you are one of many supplying the market with similar products, your only option is to drop your prices. On the other hand, if you stand out from the crowd you will be in demand, and able to increase prices. It's all about supply and demand and the relationship between these two things.

A large market may seem attractive, but if there's an even larger supply, then it's a buyer's market. On the other hand, a smaller market but with even fewer suppliers works to the advantage of suppliers. It's better to be a big fish in a small pond than a small fish in a big pond: small fish get eaten by bigger fish, and businesses without a competitive advantage fail.

Key Points

Doing what many others can do better than you is a recipe for failure. It's not what you are good at that matters; it's what you are good at that rivals aren't that gives you a competitive advantage. This competitive advantage allows you to dominate a market – even if it's a small market – and increase prices.

What to do next

- Analyse competitors through market research in order to find your competitive advantage. Choose a market that you can make your own.

- Make a list of all your competitors and note the things they can do better than you. Through a process of elimination, identify what you can do better than all (or most) of them.

See also...

13 How to make lots of enemies

Generalisation leads to competition, whereas specialisation leads to partnerships.

A generalist competes on all fronts with rivals, in each of the areas in which they're trying to win work. Being a generalist is a brilliant way to multiply the number of competitors that you have! On the other hand, a specialist business does not threaten enterprises working in complementary areas.

For example an enterprise offering website design, search engine optimisation, online videos, and copywriting is competing with all businesses working in each of those areas. In contrast, a business that focuses on the one thing at which they can excel in relation to competitors – for example by becoming a search engine optimisation specialist – can compete better in this particular field with direct rivals **and** form partnerships by offering its specialist service to other web designers, copywriters, video makers etc.

When we focus on what we excel at, we are more likely to be in our element. We know instinctively when we are doing the work we are meant to do. Great creative entrepreneurs such as fashion designer Paul Smith, product designer James Dyson and architect Norman Foster are making their unique contributions to their creative fields.

Focusing on your uniqueness is good business strategy. Celebrate and use the distinction between you and your rivals. Find a market and make it your own. Collaborate with other specialists. Do your own thing really, really well.

It is also more likely that by specialising in this way, you will be in harmony with your values and ambitions.

Key Points

By offering a wide range of services, you are competing on many different fronts. Challenging many different kinds of specialists is a great way to increase your competitors – on the other hand, by specialising, you have the option to collaborate with other specialists.

What to do next

- Decide how many other businesses you want to compete with: many or few. Open yourself up to collaborations with other businesses by specialising in what you can do best, recognising that others can do some things better than you.

- Make a list of companies you could collaborate with if you offered a speciality to complement their expertise.

See also...

14 A question from a Facebook friend

I have thousands of friends on Facebook. Not real personal friends of course, but people who connect with me only online. They befriend me through my Facebook group for creative entrepreneurs 'T-Shirts and Suits (Creativity and Business)'[8].

Early one morning, while I was waiting for my coffee to kick me awake, I logged on to Facebook and found a message from one of these friends. Marco, a young man from Italy, asked me a simple question, 'David, please tell me how I can set up a successful creative business'.

Wow, what a question!

It could take me a long time to provide a comprehensive answer to that one. So my first reaction was to ignore it completely. However, even though I didn't know Marco, I didn't want to be impolite. I decided to give him five minutes of my time providing some kind of answer. What could I usefully say in five minutes? After some thought, I found myself writing this:

Dear Marco,

1. Find something you can excel at in relation to competitors.

2. Find the customers who want this thing at which you can excel.

I hope this is useful.

Good luck!

David

Any business needs to answer these two questions. Firstly, in what field can we excel in relation to competitors? And secondly, who are the particular customers who want the things at which we can excel?

The answers to these two questions are the basic building blocks of what I call a 'unique business formula'. This is explained in detail

---

8 www.facebook.com/groups/2404983690/

in my article *Create Your Own Business Formula*[9]. Once this unique business formula is in place it becomes a blueprint for success. It also provides a solid foundation for your marketing strategy.

The unique business formula indicates a direction of travel, like a compass. Of course, a business might need to make exceptions from time to time, especially in the early days. You might need to veer off course occasionally to avoid an accident. Circumstances may force us to take some detours away from this chosen route. But at least you know the correct route. You can quickly get back on track.

These questions are not just for startups. They need to be asked and answered frequently because new competitors appear and customers' needs change over time. Ask yourself these questions at frequent intervals. At every stage in the growth of any business, the answers to these questions are crucial.

Key Points

Two questions help to devise a business formula from which a marketing strategy can be developed. In what field can we excel in relation to competitors? Who are the particular customers who want the things at which we can excel?

What to do next

• Answer these two questions now for your own business. Devise a new business formula or revise your old one. Repeat as frequently as necessary.

See also...

---

9 www.tss-cyobf.com

Slow down, you move too fast!

Instead of being a busy fool, making everyone else a rival, stop and think.

Rather than try to do everything, do one thing – or a few integrated things – really well.

Stop rushing around, sit down and answer two key questions:
(1) What can you excel at in relation to competitors?
(2) Which customers value the things you excel at?

The answers provide you with a formula for success.

And keep in tune with your values as you pursue your goals...

PART THREE

Marketing – towards what?
Goals, values and personal style

Success means different things to different people. Whatever your definition of success, it's crucial that each entrepreneur is clear about what they're trying to achieve. Your values, passion and personal style are essential ingredients within your enterprise and are intimately linked to your definition of success.

Being *authentic* in business means being true to yourself and being 'in your element'.

Identify your passions, personal style and difference from rivals. Connect these to customers who want what you can uniquely offer. Focus on what you're best at and find the customers who want that thing – strategic marketing is about finding customers who are on your wavelength. With these customers selling is easy and natural, not a painful process.

Knowing when to say NO is an essential part of a positive and focused approach to business strategy and strategic marketing.

15 Do you want to be successful?

Do you want to be successful?

That's a question I often ask audiences at my presentations about creative entrepreneurship. It's a stupid question, in one sense, because of course everyone wants to be successful. What I find very interesting though, is that everybody defines success differently. The word 'success' has generally come to mean purely financial success, but when I press people to describe their version of success in all its different aspects, their answers differ.

For some people, success **does** mean purely financial success, as quickly as possible, with no other considerations – but in fact those people are quite rare in my experience. For most people success is a matter of combining financial success (long term financial security and short term disposable income), and a range of other factors. These might include, for example, job satisfaction or a feeling of making a positive difference. Some people prioritise combining work and other aspects of life harmoniously, or freedom to choose clients and projects. Important for some is the recognition and the respect of their peers. And there are many other ingredients. Everyone wants to bake the cake of success but each person uses different ingredients, combined in different measures.

When working as a management consultant I ask my clients to define success, in their own specific terms, very clearly. In fact, I don't simply ask them, I demand it of them. Because if they are not absolutely clear where they want to go, then I cannot help them to get there.

Clarity of goals is crucial for business success. Consequently it is vital that business partners share the same goals and definition of success. Being clear about the destination is not the same thing as being clear about the route. I'm not saying that we must plan every step of the way. That's much more difficult, given that we have to take into account various challenges and detours we will have to make on the journey. Nevertheless we can be clear about where we want to end up, even if the route we eventually take to get there is irregular, bumpy and hazardous.

One creative technique I suggest to my clients is to picture themselves in the future, enjoying the success they deserve. Then, from this future point, they should look back at the key decisions they made along the way that made the difference in getting to where they have arrived. They will not remember every single detail, but they will remember the main milestones and turning points. These will be different for every business, of course, but will always be major steps. They might be strategic alliances, international growth, rebranding, forming subsidiary companies, deciding to focus on a particular product line, withdrawing from certain markets, restructuring the business, or other key matters. Returning to the present, these major steps map out the route to success.

What is your own definition of success?

Key Points

Success means different things to different people. Whatever their definition of success, it's crucial that each entrepreneur is clear about what they're trying to achieve.

What to do next

- Define success in your own terms. Picture yourself in a successful future. What does it look like? What are the key measures of success? What did you do to get there?

- Write down your definition of success, including measurable results, for a specific date in the future.

See also...

14 A question from a Facebook friend   *39*

16 Values, passion and personal style

It is important that business owners grow their businesses in a way that is consistent with their own values. This is not only a matter of personal satisfaction; it's good for business.

When advising a business, or deciding whether or not to invest in a business, I try to understand the personal passion of the business owners, their motivation, their creative passion and personal beliefs. In managing them, I would want to steer the business in a direction consistent with their values, enthusiasms and energy. Partly, this is because I want them to be happy and motivated, but also because it is good for the business. In this case there's no conflict between doing what is good for the people involved and making good business sense. Innate passion will help the business succeed through the difficult times and will be an extra source of energy when needed. This passion should also be nurtured. For the sake of the business, I want to connect this passion with the most appropriate projects, goods, services, and customers that match those interests. Anything else could undermine the energy of the business owners to the detriment of the business itself.

Deciding what **not** to do is part of any business strategy and can also be a matter of business ethics, personal values, cultural considerations and other factors.

The art of strategic management is to align the competences and passions inside the business with external markets that are on the same wavelength. These are customers with whom the business can make the best connections.

Key Points

Your values, passion and personal style are essential ingredients within your enterprise and are intimately linked to your definition of success.

What to do next

- Analyse your values, passion and personal style. You know them because they are part of you. But I suggest you actually write them down. This will help clarify your definition of success and your business formula.

- Write a list of things that conflict with your values. This list could include particular clients, projects, investors or management practices.

See also...

17 Your difference is your strength

Rob Kinsey attended one of my workshops on business development in Derbyshire, England. Rob is an artist who's also passionate about motocross, having raced motorbikes, and remains involved in the motocross world. He came to my business development workshop to find out how he might diversify his work away from his passion of motocross art in order to 'hedge his bets'. He wanted to have the ability to sell a greater variety of paintings to a wider range of clients.

By the end of the workshop he had changed his mind.

Instead of diversifying away from his passion, he decided to concentrate on it, painting exclusively motocross art and focusing on customers in that sport. Within a year, Rob was invited to exhibit his paintings at the international motocross championships in North America. There he was fêted; he was in his element; he was amongst the most enthusiastic customers for his work. And he sold many paintings.

Tessa, a young graphic designer in London, whom I advised, was enthusiastic about designing websites that in her eyes were not only functional but also of high artistic merit. They were so artistic that other people commented (sometimes not wholly in a complimentary way) that they were 'pretty' websites. She told me that other business advisers had recommended that she must diversify. They said she must be able to turn our hands to all kinds of designs, not just 'pretty websites'. She could understand what they meant but this advice nevertheless went against the grain. Deep inside her, it felt wrong.

My own advice was different.

Instead of diversifying and competing with thousands of other website designers, I suggested that she should focus on designs about which she was passionate and which were consistent with her own personal style of creativity. She should focus on her competitive advantage. She told me that this felt right and was happy to hear my distinctive advice. But working with your passions in itself does not win customers – we also need to address the question of how and from where she should win new clients.

A complete business formula needs to link a product speciality with customers who want that speciality.

So the next stage of my consultancy was to explore with her which particular types of customers might want her particular style of highly artistic website design.

Obviously, not all businesses want pretty websites, and nor should they. On the other hand, some businesses would definitely want her designs – she spoke of florists, hairdressers, clothing boutiques, beauty salons and other types of business. Coincidently, she said, these were the kinds of businesses she had dealt with so far. I wasn't surprised. She was happy to work with them but felt that she needed a wider range of customers. Other people had said that she must diversify. That's why she was asking me for marketing advice. She was, in effect, asking me how could she sell her particular style to **all** kinds of customers.

I changed the question to this: instead of trying to sell to everyone, how can we identify and win customers who want the kind of designs she excels at?

As a result, she approached the 'right kind' of customers for her work and built a business in those sectors. She didn't try to do everything. She focused on what she could do well and the customers who wanted what she did well, deliberately and positively saying no to other kinds of businesses.

For both Rob and Tessa, there was no conflict in the end between their passion, marketing, and business success. Indeed, these elements were tightly connected within a marketing strategy that works for them and their chosen customers. They are not alone. They are not even unusual. Like many successful businesses they are true to their passions and work within a marketing strategy that connects their authentic selves with the right kind of customers.

Key Points

Connect your passions, personal style and difference to customers who want what you can uniquely offer. Don't try to do everything. Focus on what you are best at and find the customers who want that thing.

What to do next

• Don't diversify, specialise. What is your real passion and speciality? Which particular kind of customers want the speciality you are passionate about?

• Write down what you are passionate about, what you can specialise in, and what makes you different from your rivals. Then list the customer types who particularly want your speciality.

See also...

18 Positive strategy involves deciding what not to do

What do fashion design guru Sir Paul Smith and motocross artist Rob Kinsey have in common? They both decline projects that don't fit with their highly selective business strategy.

In an interview on Bloomberg TV, Paul Smith explained that he says no to many projects and clients, selecting only those that suit his brand and creativity. Rob Kinsey, the specialist motocross artist, took a strategic decision not to use his talents in areas of art that he couldn't dominate, but decided to focus all his energies on a market he knew and was passionate about. He is now the top artist in his chosen field.

Apple takes the same focused approach in rejecting many potential products because they're not game changers, merely brilliant. Bill Gates, with his tremendous wealth, could have invested in all sorts of other industry sectors over the years but instead focused entirely on software. These examples all demonstrate strategic purpose and involve a tremendous amount of restraint.

As a matter of strategy, one of the most important things is to decide what **not** to do in deciding how to grow and develop our businesses. This is particularly difficult. It's especially difficult for 'busy fools'. In terms of marketing, deciding what not to do includes key strategic decisions about what products and services we should **not** offer, with which competitors we should **not** fight, and which markets we should **not** enter.

To some ears, this may sound negative, but actually it's a matter of being smart. It's all about picking our fights, finding our own particular niche, working to our strengths, and serving only the most profitable customers. It's therefore actually a very positive approach.

As a marketing consultant I often ask a new client which markets they're trying to sell to. If I hear the answer: 'all of them,' my heart sinks, because this response indicates a lack of strategy. Enthusiasm yes, strategy no. On the other hand, I am deeply impressed by an answer that indicates careful selection of customers and projects.

This tells me that the business has objectively considered its options and decided only to compete in the markets in which it can be highly successful and profitable. Such a business selects markets in which it can have an impact, working only on projects and with clients that will enhance its brand.

The difference between the unstrategic business and its strategic rival is that the first is unfocused and undisciplined whereas the second has clarity and restraint. The first will probably fail and the second one will much more likely succeed.

The most difficult thing about focusing is deciding what **not** to do. It's easy to say we will focus on this, that and the other. Focusing on 17 different things is not being focused! Even chasing two rabbits is too much; we have to let one go in order to catch the other. Letting go frees up vital scarce resources to dominate one particular market segment.

We must avoid the temptation to try and please everybody.

In fact, saying a big positive YES to chosen customers necessarily involves moving resources away from others who are less of a priority. In other words, we have to say no to some in order to say yes to others, so we might as well do it deliberately and consciously, rather than half-heartedly. Indeed by being absolutely clear about our business strategy and marketing priorities, we can both alienate and embrace customers. That is to say, we can deliberately turn away some customers and at the same time have a closer and more effective relationship with the right ones.

In my own consultancy and training business, I took a decision to say No to clients outside of the creative and digital sector, which meant that I had more capacity to help design, media and technology businesses. Consequently I further increased my expertise and reputation in my chosen sector.

Business strategy is a marketing issue, because at the heart of business strategy are the crucial decisions about which types of customers to focus on and consequently, which **not** to focus on.

A key marketing issue is to decide which markets we should **not** compete in. Strategic marketing is at the heart of business strategy.

Clearly, decisions about marketing strategy need to be reviewed from time to time because customers' needs, the competitiveness of rivals, and market conditions all change over time.

Key Points

Saying no is an essential part of a positive and focused approach to business strategy and strategic marketing.

What to do next

- Prioritise markets to identify those you can dominate and make a strategic decision to focus on these important few. Then positively say no to the rest so you can concentrate your limited resources on the right things.

- Write a list of the markets that it is possible for you to dominate. Then select the most important few from this list.

See also...

19 What does growth mean?

I was invited to meet the owners of a large design business in the south of England. When I arrived I saw that the car park was full of sports cars. Clearly this was a successful business, I thought, so I wondered how I would be able to help them. I asked the Chief Executive about the strategy they had adopted to build the business over the last ten years. He said that they had never had a strategy, they just grew organically, responding to demand, employing more people, and finding bigger offices every few years. The owners had grown the business without designing its development, and then found that the business was no longer working well. The owners told me in confidence how unhappy they were. The directors were trapped inside a business that no longer gave them job satisfaction, nor significant financial rewards.

Imagine a builder who builds a house over a period of years, brick by brick, window by window, and then when fixing the final tile in the roof realises that he has designed a house without a door. He is trapped inside. What a stupid builder! Even if the building project were a slow process, the builder would begin with a blueprint, so that every action took him in the direction of his vision for the building.

Ironically, the designers who built their design company did not do this. They were too busy putting brick upon brick (so to speak), day by day, with their heads down – never looking up to see what a monstrosity they were building. They never used their design skills to devise a blueprint for their business.

I'm not impressed by this kind of unthinking, unstrategic growth. When asked why they're growing their businesses, many owners simply say that is because that's what you should do, or that bigger is obviously better. But to me, that's not a good enough reason.

Please don't misunderstand; I'm not against business growth. I'm against unthinking, unstrategic business growth.

I don't advocate growth for growth's sake, because this often ends in failure. I have far more respect for those businesses that have decided to achieve a certain size and then to stop, than those that keep growing without knowing why. Indeed those who stop growing in terms of number of people usually have a deliberate strategy – which includes further profitable development, but not necessarily employing more staff. These businesses grow profits, not costs.

Growth is important. But what kind of growth? Business growth has become such a mantra that I fear that many businesses grow unthinkingly – I see many businesses that have grown to a particular size without having a clear strategy to do so. They've grown organically, and then find themselves in an awkward position, between a rock and a hard place. They are neither big enough to achieve the economies of scale they need to compete with larger rivals, nor small enough to be boutique, and dominate one niche. They end up with neither the agility of smallness nor the power of size.

'Turnover is vanity, profit is sanity', as the saying goes. This phrase often comes to mind when I sit watching business presentations that show turnover growing year-on-year. So what? I'm more interested in the profits behind the turnover. Some people seem to have such an obsession with turnover that they lose focus on profitability.

Personally, I'd rather have a business with £10 million turnover and 15% net profit, than a bigger business with £20 million turnover and 5% net profit. What about you? In some industries, it's very easy to increase turnover without increasing profit margin or even absolute profit. For example, advertising agencies can spend clients' money on buying TV advertising slots in such a way that the amount of money going **through** the business increases dramatically. Yet they keep very little of it. One managing director reflected on this when talking to me during a consultancy assignment. He said that he felt as though a torrent of money was going straight through his business like a powerful waterfall, and his job was to try to catch some of it for himself.

So let's be clear what we mean about growth. As the management guru Charles Handy once asked: how does growth apply to the London Symphony Orchestra? Does growth mean taking on scores of new violinists, cellists etc.? Or, more appropriately, maybe growth should mean increasing the quality of their musicians and performances so that the orchestra can attract the best conductors in the world, be commissioned to undertake world-class concerts and recordings, increase the value of its brand, build its recognition, and consequently its ability to earn income.

Similarly, we need to be clear within our own business what growth should actually mean. In contrast to other management consultants who see growth as a matter of building their businesses, employing more people, and having bigger offices, my own personal ambitions for growth are not about number of employees. I am focused on the growth of my knowledge, my reputation, and my international scope, I want to increase the impact of my consultancy projects and my training workshops. I aim to grow the market for my books. I want to increase the positive impact I have helping entrepreneurs to become even more successful. And, as a consequence of growing these things, my income also increases.

Profits can continue to grow, and significantly, by choosing the right strategy. Such a strategy might involve specialisation, focusing on particular lucrative markets, or creating joint ventures. In other words, growth can involve more than merely the size of the business in terms of employees, or even in terms of turnover.

Small can be beautiful. It can also be highly profitable.

Key Points

The wrong kind of growth can often lead to business failure. Don't grow unthinkingly. Instead decide exactly what aspects of your business you want to grow.

What to do next

• Review your business development plans and identify precisely what you want to grow.

• List the things you want to grow, together with measurable targets and a deadline for achieving each of them.

See also...

Now you can enjoy building a business in tune with your values, your passions and your own definition of success.

It's not only good for you – it's good for your business!

Integrating your values with your business strategy creates a harmony and energy that drives the business.

Say No to the things that might disturb this harmony or block positive energy.

Grow you business – by growing the right things in the right way.

And grow in partnership with only the right customers...

PART FOUR

Choosing the right customers
Why you shouldn't try to sell to everyone

Some customers are far more important than others. Not all customers are good customers. Bad customers can waste your time and cause stress. We have to find good customers and lose the bad ones. Quickly.

Marketing is about keeping great customers, not just winning new ones. Choosing the right customers is about quality as well as quantity.

Your ideal customers may not be local ones. Think globally and be prepared to expand overseas at an early stage. Exporting isn't just for big corporations.

20 Not all customers are good customers!

Customers can be bad for all sorts of reasons. They can be unprofitable or troublesome. They can waste your time or cause stress. Some interfere too much. Some aren't worthy of including in your portfolio. Others pay late, or never.

Some customers are simply more trouble than they're worth. In time, with experience, we learn to recognise such customers upfront and avoid them. But we can only avoid them if we have a choice. Businesses that are struggling financially don't have this choice and are then forced to take any kind of customer, even the bad ones. I don't want this for my clients, so we need to organise the business in a better way. By devising the correct marketing strategy we can attract the right kind of customers and deter the wrong ones. Then we can afford to say no to the wrong kind of customers because we have an abundant choice of good ones. That's the position we want to be in, but we need to work to get there. It's not just about effort and perseverance; it's about smart thinking. We need to think strategically about our business, its formula, and its carefully selected market segments.

Don't simply accept any customer!

We need to say NO to the wrong kind of customers – the customers we would decide not to work with if we could pick and choose. This creates space for the right kind of customers. We can then work with customers that are profitable and a pleasure to serve: customers and projects that add positively to our portfolio and enhance our reputation. At this point, it just gets better and better! It's an upward spiral with profits, reputation and satisfaction reinforcing each other. But first we need to avoid the opposite danger, the downward spiral. This is where a business is so desperate for customers that they will serve any 'monkey with a cheque book'.

Businesses in this position are desperate for cash and literally cannot afford to say no. Consequently they accept business from customers they can't satisfy. They might accept a contract even if it's unprofitable – as a result the business loses more money. And maybe they then do work which is not of a high quality, jeopardising their reputation. It gets worse and worse. What a nightmare.

My analysis of enterprises in this position is that they have a flawed business formula, and no effective marketing strategy. Sometimes, the underlying cause is that they are competing on price, offering services or goods that many rivals also offer. In other words, they have no speciality: they can't dominate any niche. They are drowning and grasping at straws. The only way out of this desperate position is to find something they can offer that rivals can't. They need to focus on market segments that want their speciality – and devise a marketing strategy based on competitive advantage. Without this, the business will fail.

I do understand that in the early stages of a business entrepreneurs can find themselves in the difficult situation where the business doesn't yet have a reputation and cash is tight. They need to devise a strategy, using a combination of strategic thinking and experimentation, and quickly. This difficult period should be regarded as a phase of market research – many successful businesses look back on this period as a time when they were quickly learning how to survive. They were exploring how to compete. From the lessons learned they derived a business strategy. Sadly, others will look back on this period as a horrible stressful time that led to business failure.

A bad customer isn't a bad person; they are simply not the right kind of customer for our business because they don't fit our marketing strategy. We don't have to be rude in saying no to the wrong kind of customer. In fact they might be the right kind of customer for another business with a different strategy. By referring them to another business that can serve their needs better than we can results in a win-win-win.

The difference between success and failure is a matter of marketing strategy. It's not about perseverance, creativity, or operational marketing flair. Without an effective marketing strategy the enterprise is doomed to failure.

Key Points

The wrong customers will harm your business by paying too little, too late or not at all. Bad customers can also waste your time and cause stress. We have to quickly find good customers so we can lose the bad ones. Finding good customers is a product of your business formula and marketing strategy.

What to do next

- Reflect on unprofitable customers you have dealt with and analyse the circumstances in which you dealt with them. Were you desperate for cash? Were you competing on price instead of a speciality? Decide what you need to do to be able to say NO to bad customers in the future.

- List five unprofitable projects or customers. Write down what went wrong with each of them and how you will avoid the same problem in the future.

See also...

21 How many customers do you need?

Much operational marketing energy is used trying to win customers. But first we should ask ourselves: how many customers do we need?

The first response of my clients is often 'as many as possible'. They think it's a stupid question, but it's serious. Depending on the nature of your business, you might need only ten clients, from whom you can achieve repeat business over many years. At the other end of the spectrum are businesses that require thousands, if not millions, of consumers to buy from them annually. Most businesses, of course, fall somewhere between these two extremes.

So how many customers does your business need?

Kevin Kelly wrote an article entitled 1,000 true fans[10], making the point that many individual artists and musicians can build a good business for themselves with only 1,000 fans. Crucially they must be **true fans**. These are people who follow them loyally. They are prepared to pay not only for a single MP3 download, but also want to attend concerts, buy promotional material, limited edition CDs etc. These are superfans.

Focusing on a relatively small number of extremely good customers can be a highly effective strategy. This approach can be far more successful than trying to target hundreds of thousands of lukewarm customers.

This question about the number of customers brings up the issue of the 'lifetime value of the customer'. A customer's lifetime value measures the potential for repeat business and the forecasted income from any individual customer over a long period of time. They say that it's five times easier and five times more profitable to win new business from an existing customer than to gain a new customer. (I'm not sure why they say it's five – indeed, in my opinion, the number can be much larger than this. Nevertheless, it's a good rule of thumb to remember.)

---

10 http://blog.davidparrish.com/tshirts_and_suits/2008/03/1000-true-fans.html

I invite my consultancy clients to consider the potential for winning more business from existing and past clients. It's not what they expect. They think that marketing is just about how to win totally new clients, because it's often seen as a clever and glamorous process of converting complete strangers into clients. But marketing also involves keeping existing clients. It's about selling more to the current client base and winning repeat business. It's about valuing clients who already know, like, and trust us.

I believe in working smarter, not harder. Marketing doesn't have to be difficult if we take an intelligent approach. Keeping a great customer still counts as marketing. It's not cheating – marketing isn't just about winning new customers.

I remember one occasion when I fell into the trap of allowing the glamour of winning new customers to override the good sense of looking to existing customers for additional business. Several years ago I received an email from Singapore inviting me to deliver some training workshops on strategic change management. This was unexpected and a pleasant surprise, and made me realise that there might be many other clients out there in distant exotic lands. It encouraged me to follow up various contacts and make fresh approaches to potential clients in several other countries. It was an exciting time and in many ways good fun to anticipate the prospect of much more international work. As it happened, at the same time, one of my most important clients was ready to invest in some new projects I could deliver, including training courses and business advice. But I was too busy looking elsewhere to notice. It was as if, figuratively speaking, I was looking through binoculars at the glittering lights of exotic lands, whilst a trusted client, standing right next to me, was tapping me on the shoulder and waving a wad of cash. I was brushing him away because of my enchantment with the prospect of future business elsewhere. I did come to my senses in time and took on the extra work with my existing client. Later I did indeed work in many exotic locations overseas as well.

Finding the right customers is about quality as well as quantity. Great customers can be profitable over a long period provided we look after them. How many great customers do you need?

Key Points

Marketing is about keeping great customers, not just winning new ones. Think about the potential lifetime value of each customer, not just the number of customers. Choosing the right customers is about quality as well as quantity.

What to do next

- List your existing customers in order of sales value to date. Also rank them in terms of estimated lifetime value of each client. Prioritise and focus on the important few, not the trivial many.

- From this process, select a small number of customers from whom you can get more business. Focus on these instead of trying to win new customers.

See also...

22 The important few

Some customers are more important than others. In fact, a few of your customers are probably far more important than all the rest put together. This natural imbalance is at the heart of business. Not all things are equal – there are the important few and the trivial many. Customers, products, distribution channels, staff, suppliers etc. In each category, a small number are disproportionately important.

Pareto analysis is often referred to as the 80:20 rule. This refers to a ratio where 80% of results are derived from just 20% of sources. For example, 80% of sales come from 20% of customers. Or 80% of profits come from 20% of product lines. 80:20 are good numbers to remember, but in fact this imbalance can be even more pronounced and in my experience it often is. It could be that 98% of profits are generated from just 4% of customers. The fundamental point made by such analyses is that **not all things are equal**; some things are much more important than others. Or we can say 'the important few and the trivial many'. Having recognised this, we can concentrate our efforts on the important few. For example: the top few customers; the most successful products; or the most lucrative markets.

There is a tendency to want to even things out, so that the business is not quite so dependent on a few important customers. It can be scary to have all your eggs in one basket. It would be nice to have business spread equally across many customers instead of it being weighted towards a few big ones. But it just isn't so; reality is uneven. You can fight against this tide or go with it. The important few are important for a reason – capitalise on this advantage.

Instead of directing marketing communications to all customers equally, we can focus on the most important customers. It's worthwhile to treat these special customers separately, with their own tailored marketing messages. In fact, for the most important customers you could say something really special. They're worth it.

Don't just say something special to these important customers, do special things for them. In fact, build your whole business around these important customers. They will love it. And they will love your business. These important customers are at the heart of your business – and its success.

Key Points

Not all customers are equal. Some are far more important than others. Recognise this and allocate resources accordingly.

List your special customers, and then treat them especially well.

What to do next

- Analyse customers in terms of importance. Then focus attention on the important few. Also analyse the most important products, projects, suppliers etc.

See also...

23 Location, location, location…

When I was the managing director of a specialist literary book distribution and marketing company, we expanded the business internationally, because the particular publishers we needed were located around the world, not only in the UK. In some ways it seemed quite audacious that a relatively small UK company like ours was doing business in the USA and Europe. But that's where our suppliers and customers were located.

My clients too have grown their international trade based on finding the right kind of customers for the specialist creative products they offer. For example, a film company from Liverpool won a contract in Australia. All of a sudden they no longer had to deal with customers only in their own region – the experience was a turning point that completely changed the outlook of the business, and its ambitions.

Many other businesses I have advised, especially in design, media, and technology, have also grown in this way. They have lucrative customers in more than one country. They sell their specialist services to clients who need those specialities. They don't compromise their speciality for the convenience of selling to nearby customers.

Similarly, my own small consultancy and training company has worked with clients in over 30 countries across five continents. That's because the demand for my specialist marketing and management consultancy is global, not local.

Good customers may not be conveniently located. Many businesses assume that they must first establish themselves locally. Then, as they grow, expand geographically throughout their region or country. Later, when they are large and well established, they might sell to clients overseas. This classic way of thinking may match some textbook case studies. However it doesn't fit with my experience of helping creative and digital businesses worldwide. Every business is different, of course, but most don't follow this classic pattern. And it doesn't fit with my own experience as an entrepreneur.

You don't have to be a large corporation in order to work internationally. It's a matter of finding your ideal customers, wherever they are. Don't restrict yourself to a particular geographic location and imperfect customers.

For me, Copenhagen was an ideal place to be when I spoke at the international finals of the Creative Business Cup[11]. That's because the audience corresponded precisely with my target markets: creative and digital enterprises from all around the world together with the specialist agencies that support them.

Marketing isn't about forcing the wrong customers to like what you do because they are nearby. It's about finding the customers who love what you do – wherever they are.

Key Points

Your ideal customers may not be local ones. Think globally and be prepared to expand overseas at an early stage. Export isn't just for big corporations.

What to do next

• Depending on your business, think about where ideal customers are located. Give up trying to convince bad customers just because they're conveniently located.

• Make a list of the best ten customer types for your business, irrespective of their location.

See also...

---

11 www.tss-creativebusinesscup.com

24 Niche marketing, not mass marketing

Chris Anderson, author of the *Long Tail*, made the point that it's no longer appropriate to think of mass-markets but instead 'a mass of niches'. He's right. Consumers now have more choice than ever before. Products can be differentiated to an infinite degree. Products are changing significantly from physical to digital. We need to accept his analysis and recognise the mass of niches. In my view this is exciting because every businesses can dominate its own specialist niche.

It means that even a small business can be a 'big fish in a small pond'. Or, more precisely, even as a small fish, you can still be the biggest fish in a tiny pond. You might even have a monopoly in this tiny pond, which is a great position to be in from the point of view of the supply and demand relationship between you and your customers, and hence pricing.

Discussing this with creative entrepreneurs, sometimes they say that in a tiny pond there aren't many customers. But maybe there are enough for you to achieve the success you have defined. It comes back to the question – how many customers do you actually need?

Mass marketing techniques can be seductive. There are many examples of mass marketing that we read about in the press, business books, or see for ourselves as consumers. However, we must beware of being seduced by mass marketing techniques, especially if we ourselves are managing small and medium-sized businesses. Such techniques are probably not appropriate, even in a scaled-down form. Indeed, we must think through for ourselves from the point of view of our own businesses what is the most effective marketing strategy, rather than copy inappropriate techniques.

Effective marketing is about precision. *Strategic marketing helps you find the precise customers you can serve profitably*. The marketing communications can be precisely tailored to specific niches of customers. Choose customers carefully. Think quality not quantity.

Make tailored approaches to the right kind of customers, instead of employing a scattergun approach to many potential clients.

Work smart, not hard. Find a market niche and make it your own.

Key Points

Products are more differentiated than ever and consumers have abundant choices. So we need to regard the market as a mass of niches. Choose your niche and dominate it.

What to do next

- Avoid the temptation to use a scattergun approach to address several niches at once. Be more precise. Find niches you can dominate.

- Identify one niche where you can be the go-to supplier.

See also...

25 Why 'raising your profile' is a waste of time

For goodness sake don't let me hear you talk about 'profile raising', because in my view this means scattering around information, willy-nilly, in a clueless way. It also indicates to me that you don't have a marketing strategy. It tells me that you haven't got a clue about your competitive advantage, and it says you don't know who your most suitable customers are. That's why you just do some general advertising, get some free pens made with your company's name on it, or write your business name on the side of your car in the hope that somebody somewhere will see it and magically become a customer. It's aimless and hopeless. It ain't big and it ain't clever! Rant over.

Instead, be focused.

George was an architect who needed more clients. He spent a lot of money promoting his business in a general way, ie not focused on any particular customer. For example he bought promotional pens and gave them out at random, he commissioned umbrellas emblazoned with his company logo and he had the name of his company written on the side of his car. His neighbours noticed but no new clients did. I asked him if he would pay a commission to an agent to win him a lucrative contract with an ideal customer. He agreed that he certainly would. So I suggested that instead of spending money on promotional gimmicks he invested the cash in a targeted approach to this ideal customer. He took my advice and won a contract.

Not all customers are good customers. Identify your ideal customers and use your limited resources making quality approaches to fewer targets. Focus. Don't overlook your existing and past customers in the excitement of the chase. And how do you know who your ideal customers are? Well, to be clear about that, you need to do some thinking. Think about your position in the marketplace, your competitors, how you can outmanoeuvre your rivals using your competitive advantage. Find customers who want what you can uniquely offer. In other words, you need to focus on strategic marketing. So stop being busy, stop trying to please everybody. Sit down and start thinking.

Key Points

Profile raising is a euphemism for unfocused, general marketing communications, undertaken because the business hasn't identified precise markets to target more effectively.

What to do next

- If you find yourself or a colleague suggesting activities to 'raise your profile', ask the question: With which precise customers does our marketing strategy tell us it would be profitable to have a higher profile? If there is no answer to this question it's probably because you don't have a marketing strategy. So devise one.

- Promise yourself to always communicate with specific target customers, not the general market.

See also...

Now, having let the bad customers go, we can spend more time on the good ones.

It's easier to keep a customer than to win a new one, so treat good customers well, make better products for them and increase your sales to them.

And it gets better: customers who truly value your products will pay the right price...

PART FIVE

The price of marketing
How to set the right prices

Pricing is about two things: the economic transaction and a statement of value. Pricing influences customers' perception and view of quality. A high price can reassure customers about quality and may actually **increase** sales.

If you find you have to drop your prices or change your product to what rivals offer, it probably means you're dealing with the wrong kind of customers. Instead, find the right customers – the ones who are prepared to pay the full price for what you can uniquely offer. We need to focus our businesses on things we can do that rivals cannot. This will enable us to increase prices – with the right kind of customers.

Only when we fully understand how valuable the benefits of our products are to the customer can we price accordingly.

26 Increase prices – to lose customers!

I suggest you increase your prices dramatically and, hopefully, you'll lose some customers!

That's fine. Because the customers you will lose are not in love with you, just your low prices. The ones you will not lose are those who really want to buy from you, because you're better than the alternatives on offer. In other words, you'll retain customers on the basis of your competitive advantage. They value the way you are distinctive.

Pricing policy goes hand-in-hand with selecting the right kind of customers. By increasing prices you can deter the wrong kind of customers, which is half the battle. Increasing prices *forces us* to find the right kind of customers. In fact, increasing prices forces us to make strategic decisions.

When working as a management consultant with my clients I sometimes set up the following scenario as a way of thinking through the development of an effective and profitable marketing strategy. I play the role of the new owner of my client's business – and dictate to them that as from today they must increase prices threefold. That's a command, not a suggestion. The first reaction of my client is despair – they know they'll lose many customers and are unsure how to win customers who will buy at the new price level. Still acting in the role of a dictatorial boss, I tell them to come back in three weeks time with new customers, who will buy at the new price level. This means that the business is forced to differentiate itself from competitors, to play to its strengths, to find the market niches in which it can have a near-monopoly, and to avoid those products or services that rivals can also offer. It forces the business to identify its competitive advantage and find the customers who want what it can uniquely offer.

Often a client's reaction to this imposed price increase is to say: 'Nobody around here will pay that price!'

To that, my response is: 'Then don't sell to customers around here!'

Perhaps the best market for our products isn't local. We need to challenge the assumption that our current market base is the correct one.

Another response is that with a higher price, sales will drop. That's okay I say – at a higher price we don't **need** to sell as many. Perhaps we can make more profit from fewer sales, but at a higher price. Again this provokes question about profitability.

Most importantly though, by imposing a price increase in this way, the team managing the business is forced to address the issue of how on earth it can compete with rivals. You have to find something of value that rivals can't offer to be able to justify the higher price to customers. You have to make sure you have some point of difference that competitors can't replicate, and that customers value. You have to distinguish yourself from the crowd, and find customers who value that distinctiveness.

If, after due consideration and research, we simply can't answer the question of what will justify a higher price, it means that we are coming to a worrying conclusion about the ability of the business to compete. Perhaps we're selling a near-commodity – we are not really any different than our competitors, and consequently we are condemned to competing on price. The only way to proceed if this is the case is to drive down costs, keep prices as low as possible, and increase sales to compensate for loss of profit margin. Competing on price in this way can be done, but it's not ideal.

On the other hand, if we can identify something at which we excel in relation to competitors – if we can differentiate ourselves in a way that customers value – then we've found our competitive advantage. At this point we are half way to success. The next stage is to find those customers who want or need the particular thing at which we can excel.

So, put up your prices, because this will deter the wrong kind of customers. It won't deter customers who really want what you can uniquely offer. This change of prices will influence your market positioning and the perception of customers – it could be an opportunity to refine your marketing communications, or even fundamentally review your business.

A word of warning! You may not be able to increase your prices with current customers because of existing contracts or because it could jeopardise goodwill. A new pricing policy may have to be implemented only with new customers.

The question of raising prices also inevitably brings about a useful discussion about marketing strategy and indeed the underlying business strategy – the competitive advantage of a business in relation to its rivals, and the validity of its customer base.

The boardroom strategy game of imposing a significant price increase provokes a more fundamental and important exercise of finding the unique business formula. This business formula is based on the answer to two questions:

- At what can we excel in relation to competitors?

- Who are the particular customers who want the thing at which we excel?

Key Points

An imposed increase in prices would mean losing some customers – but only those who can go to cheaper rivals. We need to focus our business on things we can do that rivals can't, which enables us to increase prices – with the right kind of customers.

What to do next

- Think through what you would do if a new dictatorial boss insisted you increase prices threefold. Which customers would you lose and which would you retain? What does the result tell you about your competitive advantage? At what can you excel in relation to competitors? Who are the particular customers who want that thing at which we can excel?

- Make a list of current and potential customers who would pay **more** for what you are especially good at.

See also...

20 Not all customers are good customers!   *60*

27 You don't have to sell cheap or sell out

Lise is a fashion designer in Norway who complained that the only way she could make a decent living is to either reduce her prices or make much more ordinary products she wasn't passionate about. She felt stuck between a rock and a hard place and decided she had only two choices: *to sell cheap or to sell out.*

This is because she was dealing with the wrong kind of customers. Those inappropriate customers are often known as 'people round here'. The solution to her problem was to find new customers who actually want what she could uniquely offer and were prepared to pay the price. They may not be conveniently located in your area, but by challenging the assumption that we must sell locally, we can win on both counts. We can find customers who want our undiluted talents and are prepared to pay handsomely for them.

When you select the wrong kind of customers you either end up selling cheap, or selling out.

Often, a problem presented to me by clients as an issue of pricing or profitability is really a matter of strategic marketing. Some customers do not fully value what you can offer. Others might not want all of your expertise or products, just part of them. Consequently, they're not prepared to pay the full price. Why should they? They can probably get these elements of what you offer from other places. These customers do not suit you properly. They can shop around and go to rivals who offer what they need. Hence, they want a reduced price because they know they can go elsewhere. Do not drop your prices to win these customers because they are not the *right* customers. This is how the lack of strategic marketing can lead to you selling cheap.

As for selling out, this happens when a business responds to the needs of the wrong kind of customers. After listening to the wrong kind of customer, they alter their service or product in such way that it takes them into danger areas where rivals dominate. This is absolutely the wrong direction. Instead, we need to head for the high ground we can dominate, not be lured into competitors' territory. We need to find our own specialist niche. We will find the right kind of customers there.

This is another example of how *strategic marketing* beats *operational marketing*.

Instead of trying to use operational marketing techniques to increase prices, or convince the wrong kind of customers to buy at the right kind of price, we look at the bigger picture. Strategic marketing takes a more comprehensive view of the business. Strategic marketing may mean changing the customer base substantially.

Key Points

If you find you have to drop your prices or change your product to what others can do, it probably means you're dealing with the wrong kind of customers. Instead, find the right customers who are prepared to pay the full price for what you can uniquely offer.

What to do next

- Recognise that when you are asked to drop your price there is something wrong with your marketing strategy. It either means you're dealing with the wrong customers, or offering too generic a product. Instead, focus on what you can excel at, and find the right customers for your business.

- Resolve that when you are asked to drop your prices, the problem is not your product but your choice of customer.

See also...

28 The high price of benefits

See everything that the customers see, and then increase
your prices. Understanding customer benefits pays dividends.
By recognising the full value of our offerings, we can charge
customers accordingly.

Indeed, higher prices might actually become part of the attraction.
One of the benefits of owning a Rolls Royce is that everybody
knows they are expensive. So the ownership of a Rolls Royce is
also a signal of your wealth. This conspicuous consumption can be
a benefit too. And the same can be said for Rolex watches, private
jets, certain clothing brands and many other products that are
known to be expensive.

Listen to customers. Understand customers' points of view.
Discover everything customers value in your products. Then
price accordingly.

Key Points

Once we understand how valuable the benefits of our products are
to the customer, we can price accordingly.

What to do next

- Listen to customers to understand what they really value in
  your products.

- Question whether you are pricing your products high enough,
  given all the value the customer obtains from the benefits
  we provide.

- Scrutinise your prices and consider how they can be increased
  due to additional benefits you could offer (or are already
  delivering but not pricing in).

See also...

29 Reassuringly expensive

Stella Artois advertises its beer as 'reassuringly expensive'. I love that. They are proud of their high price. They are selling the **benefit** of a high price. And they are clearly differentiating themselves from other brands that might emphasise value in terms of low price. The term 'reassuringly expensive' puts the beer in the same league as other high-class and sought-after products. It's like saying that Stella Artois is the Rolls-Royce of beers.

Despite the law of supply and demand, a high price can actually **increase** sales.

Of course this doesn't apply to simple commodities, because nobody would pay a high price when exactly the same thing is on sale at a lower price. The point is that most products and services are **not** simple commodities such as sugar or oil or wheat. Every product and service is different in some way than its rivals or its equivalent. One computer game is not quite the same as another; one architectural service is not exactly the same as the alternative on offer; each musical performance is unique. A feature film made by one director will be different than another made to the same specification. The choice facing customers is much more complex and varied. Not only is the direct product or service different in some way, but the intangibles associated with it are also different. The status of the brand and the kudos attached to owning this – rather than that – is different. The level of service bundled with the product, even the packaging, is different. There are also differences in the sales experience, and the peace of mind resulting from choosing the 'right' thing.

There's much to play for in the game of selling benefits, customer perception, and pricing.

Are your prices set at a level to convey the same message? Consequently, do customers regard your products as in the league of Rolls-Royces – or the cheap runabout?

There's a tremendous amount of psychology involved in pricing. As mentioned above, a high price can actually be an attraction to buy. Not only can a higher price be reassuring, it can also have 'show-off value'. This is the phenomenon of 'conspicuous consumption', signalling the buyer's wealth through the purchase. The consumer is using goods and services to demonstrate publicly their ability to splash out at the top of the range.

Another pricing technique when offering a range of products at various prices is to make sure that there is at least one product with an extremely high price. The purpose of this is not necessarily to sell that product but to make the other prices look quite reasonable in comparison. For example, a wine list will often include a very expensive bottle of wine. It may be that the restaurant doesn't even have a bottle of this particular wine available in its cellar, but that doesn't matter. The purpose of that bottle is to sell the others, and particularly to sell the more expensive wines in the range because it moves the average price upwards.

Would you like your products to be regarded as 'reassuringly expensive'?

Key Points

Pricing influences customers' perception and view of quality. A high price can reassure customers about quality and may increase sales.

What to do next

- Consider differentiating yourself from rivals through a high price policy. Which customers would be reassured by this?

- Go through your price list and consider an enhanced price for each product that would make it 'reassuringly expensive'.

See also...

38 Selling benefits   112

30 Help your retailers

Zara was running a new business selling designer wedding dresses. She had found a shop that was willing to stock her products and was very excited about this opportunity. She also told me that the owner of the shop had agreed to take less of a profit on her dresses than on those she sold from other suppliers. Zara explained that she couldn't afford to offer a significant profit to the retailer, and hoped that she understood the situation. The retailer did understand and kindly agreed to sell her dresses anyway. But the pricing policy meant that there was less financial incentive for the shop owner to sell her dresses, than those of her rivals, so she didn't promote them strongly, and certainly didn't put Zara's wedding dresses in her shop window; they were left at the back of the shop. Sales were disappointing.

My advice was to change the situation around, and increase the retail price of the dresses so that the retailer made a handsome profit. Now there was a clear financial incentive for the shop owner to promote these dresses – she put them in the window, and offered them as the first choice to customers.

When I was managing my first enterprise, a bookshop in a small town, a woman from a community group came in, asking us to sell copies of the pamphlet they had produced. The pamphlet sold at £1 and this price was actually printed on the cover. As a bookseller I asked about the discount the publisher would give us against this price. (At that time bookshops received approximately $1/3$ discount against the retail price). The person selling the pamphlets looked blankly at me and asked, 'What do you mean?' She said that they had not published the booklet to make a profit and were selling it at £1 because that was the production cost. In response, I said that usually we sold books at a higher price than we bought them (trying not to sound sarcastic). I explained that the difference between the price we bought them and sold them was how we paid our rent, other costs and our wages. There was absolutely no financial incentive for us to stock this book or to sell it. (Actually, in this instance we did stock and sell the book, taking a financial hit because we wanted to support the community group and their message. Other retailers weren't so understanding.) I advised her to think about the needs of retailers when publishing the next pamphlet.

Pricing becomes more complex if we sell our products through intermediaries in the distribution process along the way to the end user. We need to make sure the pricing policy works all along the supply chain – that it is profitable for the wholesaler and retailer to promote and sell our goods. These pricing decisions can incentivise or disincentive the business partners we depend upon to get our product to the end-user.

Key Points

If we are using distributors and retailers to sell our products, we need to ensure that they have an incentive to promote our products above the alternatives. Pricing and profitability needs to work for everyone involved in our distribution channels.

What to do next

• Find out what profit margins and incentives rivals offer to distributors and retailers. Make sure that you're not disadvantaged by offering less attractive prices and terms to them.

See also...

31 Free

Banda Calypso's music is copied onto CDs and sold on street corners in Brazil. They don't get a cut of this income but they don't mind. In fact, they supply these street-sellers with master CDs to copy! And they organise things so that there is a plentiful supply of their music for sale in each town on the route of their tour, before they arrive to perform. They see this copying and selling as an advertising function and they don't have to pay these street-corner entrepreneurs. They have turned pirates into their promoters. Their gigs are always full and they've made enough money to buy their own private jet to take the band on tour.

Timothy Chan, one of the richest men in China, used to get ripped off by copyright pirates. His computer game CDs were copied illegally and sold cheaply. He could have tried in vain to stop this. Or he could have let his business go bankrupt. Instead, he changed his business to take advantage of the copying. He decided to make his money from online connection fees instead of CD sales. He changed the game so people had to play online and pay a very small fee per minute. The copied CDs spread like wildfire and so did his customer base. Every CD copied now helped his business.

Smart entrepreneurs see opportunities when others see only threats. They change their business models to take advantage of changing technology, economics and social trends.

Creative entrepreneurs often ask me how they can make money from their music or computer games, when MP3 files and software is so easy to copy. One answer is to use the fact that people copy your stuff to change a threat into an opportunity. Ironically, one discount that can be highly effective in some circumstances is a discount of 100%. Giving things away for free can be a part of a winning marketing strategy.

In his book *Free!*, Chris Anderson outlines 50 business strategies that involve giving something away for free. There have always been free samples and loss leaders – there are plenty of examples of giving something away for free in order to make more money through sales later. A classic example is the Gillette razor, given for free but making money on replacement razor blades. Inkjet printers aren't actually free but the main profit comes from the ink cartridges that users need to buy (frequently!) to use the printers.

Some of the most profitable computer games are 'free to play' but make big money from selling in-game purchases to a small number of superfans. Nicholas Lovell gives several examples of this in his excellent book *The Curve*.

Free is not a business strategy in itself of course, but it can be an effective part of a larger picture that in total is highly profitable.

Key Points

Giving some things away free can be part of a profitable marketing strategy.

What to do next

- Consider what you could give away free in order to increase sales of other products to make your business as a whole more profitable.

See also...

32 Invoices can state two prices

In terms of marketing, pricing is crucially important because of the signal it sends to customers about where we sit in a competitive marketplace. By choosing any price point, we send a message to customers. The price may be decided internally, within the business, for economic reasons. At the same time, the marketing perspective says that we must look at things from the point of view of the customer. And what the customer sees is not the internal financial calculations, but a price that's higher than competitor X, and lower than competitor Y.

In other words, the customer quickly makes a judgement about our products from the information *we* give them through the price. This pricing information places us, and our products, at a certain point in relation to the alternatives.

So, pricing is simultaneously about two different things:

1. The financial transaction; and

2. A message about value

Many early-stage businesses that haven't yet established a reputation – and are perhaps desperate for revenue – feel that they can't charge a high price. But by charging a low price they're sending a signal that implies that their product is not as good as the alternatives. They are actually undermining their own brand, and setting a precedent that will prevent them from increasing prices in the future. Yes it's a kind of Catch-22. Businesses often don't know what to do in this situation.

My advice is based on the understanding that pricing is about two separate things, as described above; it's about both the financial transaction and a signal of value. By recognising these two factors we can develop a dual strategy if we need to sell cheaply as a short-term tactic. The invoice supplied to a client at the point-of-sale can have two prices – or at least, it can say two things. It can say that the real value is (for example) $1,000. Then it can indicate that there is a discount **on this occasion** of 50%, for example as a goodwill gesture to a new customer, or because this is a special project. As a result of the discount, the bottom line is actually $500 and this is the amount of the financial transaction. On one invoice we have said two things. We have said that on this occasion we will sell the product for $500, but we also made absolutely clear that the real value is $1,000.

The benefits of this are several.

The first is that the customer realises that they are getting a bargain – and everyone likes a bargain! Secondly, it prevents the discounted price setting a precedent. If the customer returns for a repeat purchase they don't expect that the next sale will be $500 because, after all, this isn't the proper price. And if the customer needs reminding in the future, they can be referred to the earlier invoice that clearly states that the normal price is actually $1,000. Thirdly, when the customer recommends us by word-of-mouth we don't want them to tell their friends and colleagues that they should also expect a price of $500. What we actually want them to say about our product is that they were delighted and the true value is $1,000. This encourages others to buy at the full price. If they do happen to mention that they paid only $500, they are much more likely to also say that they were lucky enough to get an exceptional discount and the normal price is actually $1,000. In this way, we can achieve both our objectives simultaneously: a sale **and** a signal of high-value.

This is a tactic that might have to be used by early stage businesses. As soon as realistically possible we need to charge the full price consistently.

Key Points

Pricing is about two things: the economic transaction and a statement of value. If you give a discount for any reason, you should still state the full value. This is important for future reference and to ensure the customer fully values your product.

What to do next

- Make sure that any discounts don't come back to haunt you or get passed around from customer to customer. Prevent this by stating the full commercial price on all invoices, even if on occasion you don't charge it.

See also...

At this stage I hope you're feeling more confident about increasing your prices by recognising the value you offer.

Price is not a matter of confidence though; it's a matter of strategy.

By connecting to only the right customers – who want what you excel at, you can increase prices.

Next, we need to listen to those customers...

PART SIX

Don't talk to customers – listen first

Listening to customers and other market research techniques

Market research is fundamentally an attitude – a belief that we can learn useful things from customers. It needn't be a huge expensive exercise. Instead, use the term 'listening to customers' to think of practical and inexpensive ways to open up a dialogue with key customers. You will gain information and ideas to help you beat your rivals.

Ask your selected customers to share their views of your business and they will most likely tell you useful stuff you don't know, so that you can improve.

33 Don't do market research!

Marketing is all about looking at things from the customer's point of view. That requires understanding customers and, indeed, listening to customers.

Listening to customers is the term I tend to use, instead of the phrase 'market research'. That's because 'market research' tends to conjure up the idea in people's minds of very formal exercises, undertaken at huge expense by big corporations. If I suggest to smaller businesses that they undertake 'market research', their initial reaction is that it's completely out of the question, because of the cost. The term 'market research' isn't useful. So instead, I talk with clients about how they might 'listen to customers'. Using this different phrase sounds much more down-to-earth, more do-able, and much more like common sense. All of a sudden, it seems feasible to listen to what customers have to say about their needs and our products. Because the term 'listening to customers' is more accessible, we can then move on to a conversation about how this might be achieved.

Market research, or 'listening to customers', is not so much a collection of techniques and processes; more fundamentally it's an **attitude**. It's a way of thinking about customers and our relationship with them. It's a matter of acknowledging that maybe customers have something important to tell us, not only about themselves, but also about our businesses. Yes, perhaps customers know things about our business that we don't know ourselves. We have to be open to the possibility that we don't know everything, even about our own enterprises. If our attitude is complacent, assuming that we know everything there is to know about our business and customers' needs, market research will never happen. Because with this attitude there's nothing we can learn from listening to customers. Some entrepreneurs think they know it all already. They believe they simply have to talk at customers, not waste time listening to what they might have to say.

In my view that's arrogant and foolish. And it's very bad business. On the other hand, we can take an authentic interest in how customers perceive our business. We can be curious about their current and future needs. We can ask them what they really think about our products. We can be intrigued about how they see the benefits on offer from our business. We can ask about their problems and then devise solutions to those problems to sell to them. Instead of being arrogant we can be ready to listen. This is the breakthrough – from this point onwards listening to customers becomes easy, because there's a will to do so. All it requires is a genuine openness to hearing what customers might have to say. The rest is detail. From here it's just a small step to finding practical and useful ways of creating a dialogue with customers.

If you don't think customers are worth listening to, then read no further...

On the other hand, perhaps you **do** actually care what customers think. Do you want to hear new ideas and attitudes? Are you prepared to be surprised? Would you value new insights from the minds of customers? If so, then read on. With this authentic inquisitiveness, you're in an excellent position to make further steps to gain an advantage on rivals. You're on the verge of gaining a better understanding of the ways customers think, how they behave, what they want, and what they value.

At its simplest, you could phone a sample of customers to ask them about your products. You could invite a small number of customers to an informal focus group. This could be in a relaxed, informal setting, to generate discussion about their ideas, experiences, and attitude towards buying your products and those of your competitors. Simple techniques such as reply cards, short questionnaires, and online surveys might all have their place to play and can be manageable and affordable even by smaller businesses. Listening to customers can also be undertaken at the point-of-sale. Winning customers need not be a one-way process of **selling** to them and talking **at them**. It's all about taking the time to listen, showing an interest in what they think, and simply creating space for them to enter into a dialogue.

Key Points

Market research is fundamentally an attitude – a belief that we can learn useful things from customers. It needn't be a huge expensive exercise. Instead use the term 'listening to customers' to help you think of practical and inexpensive ways to open up a dialogue with key customers. You'll gain information and ideas to help you beat rivals.

What to do next

- Use the term 'listening to customers' so that market research doesn't sound out of the question but down to earth and doable. Find inexpensive practical ways to listen to customers' views, needs and ideas.

- Make a list of things you would like to find out from customers. Write down the names of ten customers. Ask them.

See also...

34 Customers know stuff we don't

Bill, a partner in a large accountancy practice, used to audit the accounts for my book distribution and marketing company, many years ago. He once told me that their firm was proud of how quickly they could prepare annual accounts and return them to their clients. I asked him if this is what their clients really wanted. He looked at me in a slightly puzzled way and reiterated how speedy they were in comparison to rival firms. 'But maybe clients aren't bothered about speed,' I said. 'Have you asked them?' A few weeks later he called me and said that they had asked a handful of clients about their speedy service. It turned out that they didn't want their accounts prepared urgently – but what they did want was for the accountants to attend a meeting of directors to present and explain the significance of the financial reports. Until Bill and his colleagues took the trouble to actually ask their clients what was important to them, they were making assumptions and priding themselves on something that was of little value to their clients.

We need to listen to customers because they know stuff about our business that we don't. Customers see things differently to us. They often see value where we don't – or don't value what we think they ought to. Marketing is about looking at things from the customers' point of view.

If we treat customers with respect by being prepared to listen to them, then they might help us. Customers can tell us what we're getting wrong; customers can tell us how we can improve; they can tell us what we are getting right that we should never change. They can tell us how we can be even more valuable to them.

This isn't obvious. Don't assume that customers value what we expect them to value. They might want something slightly different than what we're offering. We just don't know until we listen to them.

Of course, in listening to customers we must select the **right** kind of customers. As already noted: not all customers are good customers. Clearly we mustn't listen to the wrong kind of customers. And so effective market research ('listening to customers') must engage only the right kind of customers. If we ask the wrong customers we'll get the wrong answers. That means that first we need to choose customers strategically. The right customers are those who need what we can excel at, who share our values, and are prepared to pay the right price for the expertise we offer.

Key Points

Ask your selected customers to share their views of your business and they will most likely tell you useful stuff you don't know, so that you can improve.

What to do next

- Start by selecting just one important customer. Decide how best to have a dialogue with them. Ask them how they see your business and how they suggest you can improve.

See also...

35 Crowd-testing

I was privileged to share a platform at an entrepreneurship conference in Chile with Slava Rubin, the chief executive officer of the crowd funding company Indiegogo. I had already mentioned crowd funding in my speech. He added much more detail from his own experience of running one of the most successful crowd-funding platforms. Amongst many interesting things he said, he pointed out that crowd-funding platforms can be used to undertake market research. An idea at an early stage can be publicised there, in order to attract funding and investment. At the same time, it can also test the market for any particular product – in fact, two or three potential products could be publicised in order to see which one generates the most interest. If nobody's interested then that tells us something. Obviously it's better to find out bad news at this stage – rather than later – if there's simply no demand for our new product. On the other hand, we might be pleasantly surprised at the interest shown in a new project that we didn't expect to receive such a warm welcome from its market. I wrote about his insights on my blog[12].

There are now a number of crowd funding platforms that have been used successfully by creative and digital businesses, not only to successfully raise finance but to get feedback and build a customer base. It was particularly interesting to speak with staff from Kickstarter because of its range of creative projects. In New Zealand and elsewhere I learnt about new crowd funding platforms that are tailored towards the needs of local markets. They can all be useful for market research as well as raising investment.

Those people who are convinced that the new idea is bound to be a big hit will never consider such a thing. But if we take the attitude that we simply don't know everything and we need to ask customers, then this is a great way of finding out.

---

12 http://blog.davidparrish.com/tshirts_and_suits/2011/11/crowd-testing.html

Key Points

Crowd funding platforms can be a great way to test an idea at an early stage as a form of market research.

What to do next

- When considering your next products or projects, ask what customers think first. In fact, using crowd-funding platforms, ask the crowd.

See also...

36 Is it really a feasibility study?

At the end of my training workshops for entrepreneurs, people often come up to me for a private conversation. Sometimes they tell me that they have decided not to pursue their business project because of what they've learned within the workshop. Or they've decided to delay it until they've undertaken more research.

The workshop has tested the feasibility of their business idea and they've learned that it's not feasible. Or at least, it's not feasible yet. For me, this is a positive result. It's positive because it has saved the waste of resources in terms of money, energy, time and opportunity cost on behalf of the entrepreneur.

Feasibility studies can also be undertaken by listening to customers. Pilot projects can be used as short-term experiments to test a business idea.

However, the trouble with most pilot projects and feasibility studies is that they're not really open to the possibility of not continuing. So a pilot project is just a term for the initial phase of a project that someone has already decided will definitely happen anyway. A feasibility study becomes an exercise in proving to ourselves that our idea is a good one. This was the case in a major investment project I advised in the United Arab Emirates. A super-wealthy Sheik insisted that the feasibility study must report positively in order to justify the decision he had, in reality, already made.

In contrast, true feasibility studies are actually set up in order to learn something. Even if the thing to learn is that our idea is not good enough, or the demand is not strong enough. To find out this negative news is actually a positive. Surely it's better to find out at an early stage that we're about to waste scarce resources?

Pilot projects are consistent with the approach of the 'lean startup' movement and the concept of the 'minimum viable product'. Before developing a product fully with all its potential extras, it's better to test a simpler version or prototype. Or test many more products and get feedback. In this way, we learn what customers think, and find

CHASE ONE RABBIT

that what customers really want. Shockingly, this is often not what we think they ought to want.

Key Points

True feasibility studies must be open to the possibility that the idea being tested will fail. Otherwise it's not really a feasibility study. Finding that an idea doesn't work, or needs redevelopment is a positive thing. It saves resources and helps us get it right sooner.

What to do next

• Undertake feasibility studies and pilot projects with a willingness to learn that the thing being tested doesn't work. Using this open-minded market research we can more quickly develop the right things.

• Make it a policy that feasibility studies and pilot projects are allowed to 'fail'.

See also...

Listening to customers needn't be complicated.

The most difficult thing might be to change your mindset from talking at customers to listening to them.

Starting with just one customer, practice listening. Invite them for a coffee and give them a good listening to.

Then with the insights and knowledge we gain from this, you are in a better position to sell customer benefits...

PART SEVEN

What's in it for me?
Selling benefits to customers

The customer wants to know what's in it for them. They don't care about you, your business and what you find interesting about it.

What a customer gets out of a product may be very different than what we put into making it. Customer benefits may include both obvious and non-obvious elements. Benefits can be tangible or intangible. We may not fully understand the way that customers value these benefits. So ask them.

It's easy to fall into the trap of talking about our business from our own perspective (features) rather than saying what's in it for the customer (benefits). Some things matter much more to us than they do to customers. Identify these features and de-prioritise them in marketing communications. Highlight instead benefits that **do** matter to customers.

37 Nobody cares about you and your business

Jane contacted me on behalf of her community arts company to ask my advice about selling arts activities to schools. An ex-teacher, and passionate about the arts, Jane was running her own business, taking artistic projects into schools. But her sales technique wasn't working. She would bounce into the offices of head teachers, enthusing about the arts, talking passionately about music or theatre, and showing her portfolio of amazing artistic projects. To me, it was a classic case of her falling into the trap of emphasising features not benefits: talking about process and not results. She was failing to convey what these projects would do to benefit the head teacher, whom she was asking to pay for the project as a customer.

We needed to turn her sales pitch round. Instead of starting at **her** end of the story – and eventually getting to what the customer was interested in – we had to start from the customer's end. This was perfectly logical to me – and indeed to her when she thought about it rationally – but it went against the grain of her instinct, and was contrary to her passionate approach. Nevertheless, we did it. We forced ourselves to take the customer's view and imagine ourselves in the shoes of a head teacher. The head teacher would be under pressure to deliver results, as measured by the school's inspectors, whose criteria were academic achievements and the development of each individual child free from the risks of bullying, racism and sexist prejudices.

And of course the head teacher would be under pressure financially, with very little budget to spend on things perceived as unnecessary extras. Because Jane talked about 'arts activities', the head teacher classified them as something that would be 'icing on the cake' but certainly not a priority. By looking at things from the point of view of the head teachers, we recognised that we needed to solve their problems. We needed to offer them the benefit of achieving a more satisfactory inspector's report, helping them to change the culture of the school so that students could excel academically within a culture free of racism, sexism and bullying.

And so a much more effective approach started by recognising the challenges facing the school and by offering a solution.

Instead of selling the arts, we began to sell a solution to problems. We offered a number of projects that addressed the issues highlighted in the unsatisfactory inspector's report and asked the head teacher if they would be willing to invest in them. Of course they would. Jane then quoted examples of how she had achieved similar results in other schools. Now, the sales pitch was working. Eventually, head teachers started to agree that some projects were necessary and trusted Jane's company to deliver results. Only at the end of the conversation did the head teacher ask about the details of the projects, the methods, the techniques, and specifically how Jane would manage the projects in order to achieve the results required. Only now did Jane talk about the arts. Despite her passion for the arts, she recognised that – from the head teacher's point of view – the arts were simply a means to an end, not an end in themselves. Art was a feature, not a benefit.

In our enthusiasm, we talk too much.

There's a danger that we give unwanted information to the customer. I've lost count of the number of business presentations that start with the founder giving a potted history of their business: when it started, how it started, where it started. 'Get to the point!' I'm thinking, as they go through the chronology, slowly leading into the present and the real point of their presentation, which might be a sale, a bid for an award or a pitch for investment. The history is important to the business owner, and from their point of view there's a logic to starting at the beginning: how the business started; how it's developed; leading nicely into where it is now, what it's offering, and what it needs.

But who cares?

The fact is, nobody cares about you and your business. They only care about what's in it for them.

So... the audience wants it the other way around. The customer wants you to start with what's in it for them. Then, if they're interested, they might want to dig deeper and look at the history of the business, its internal workings, and other such details.

One of the most important factors in marketing communication is to make a distinction between features and benefits. There are features (facts) about a product or service that we, as the business, know well. And there are benefits – in other words, what the actual product or service will actually **do** to help, serve or delight the customer.

The customer wants to know about benefits.

And yet we persist in talking about features, because they're the things that interest **us**. We look at the product or service not through the eyes of the customer but through our own eyes. In doing so, we fail to express benefits and we can even alienate the customer.

The acid test is whether or not the customer says in response to your sales pitch: 'So what?' It's what I call the 'So What?' test of features and benefits.

We need to start from the customer's end of the story, not our own – start with benefits and talk about features only as required. Don't fall into the trap of starting with features and hoping that we get to benefits before the customer loses interest. The customer's only question is: 'What's in it for me?'

Key Points

The customer wants to know what's in it for them. They don't care about you, your business and what you find interesting about it.

What to do next

- Use as a starting point the customer's question 'What's in it for me?' and design your marketing communications to answer this question.

- Appoint a colleague to act as a surrogate customer to test all marketing communications by asking 'What's in it for me?'

See also...

38 Selling benefits

Customers see the world differently than we do. They see our products in terms of benefits to them. Sometimes they see benefits we haven't seen ourselves. Perhaps they see value where we haven't recognised it. What the customer gets out of a product may be quite different than what we put into it. There may be several benefits from the customer's point of view. This is what I call the 'bundle of benefits'.

When I go into the Apple Store to buy another accessory, there are several benefits to me. The product I purchase is the obvious one. But there are others too. My delight in the packaging, my interaction with the t-shirted sales assistant, and the cool carrier bag. At a deeper level, there's also my reaffirmation of my membership of the cult of Apple!

This bundle of benefits can include both tangible and intangible elements, obvious and non-obvious things. For example, tangibles might include the packaging, accessories, a certificate of authenticity or other things associated with the product. Intangibles might include delivery, insurance, after-care services and maintenance. Further intangible benefits might be kudos, or the ability to associate one's lifestyle with a brand. Or it might be a 'connection' with the creator. It could be membership of the community that exists around the product. A sense of community can be part of the package of benefits on offer to the customer. We are social beings and like to feel that we are part of some community, whether geographical, a 'community of interest', or even a spiritual community.

Post-sales advertising has this effect. Seeing an advert for something we've already bought doesn't encourage us to buy again, but it reassures us that what we've bought was a good choice. Having bought a particular car, we start to notice how many of them there are on the roads all of a sudden, because we feel some kind of kinship with other owners of the same model. When using wi-fi in cafes, I can't help but notice which people are using Apple laptops or non-Apple brands; I feel there's an unspoken connection between me and these other 'Apple people'. Clothing brands, alcoholic drinks, music venues, books, and a whole range of products (and often services too) have the same effect – it's the effect of helping people feel that they're part of something bigger. That something could be good taste, an economical choice, similar aspirations, or solidarity in some kind of cause.

This kind of kinship, once recognised, can be built upon and customers can be offered some kind of formal or informal membership of a community. We're social animals. In a book called *Yes! 50 stories from the science of persuasion*, there's the story of an experiment investigating people's behaviour as hotel guests, and their propensity to recycle towels. When told that recycling towels was good for the earth a certain number responded positively, but when told that 'the majority of people in this hotel recycle their towels', the response was even greater. It seems that we're more concerned with being part of the right group than we are about the future of the planet.

The bundle of benefits may include things that the customer values that we don't even know about. The only way to find out is to look at things from the customers' point of view. Talk to them and ask them.

Key Points

The benefits a customer gets out of a product may be different than what we put into making it. This bundle of benefits may include both obvious and non-obvious elements. Benefits can be tangible or intangible. We may not fully understand the way that customers value these benefits. So ask them.

What to do next

- Find ways of understanding how customers value the benefits of your products, both tangible and intangible. Talk to customers about these benefits and how they value them.

- If possible, visit five customers to find out how they're actually using your product or service, with a view to finding additional customer benefits you may have been unaware of.

See also...

39 Barking up the wrong tree

James and his wife own and manage an art gallery in South Africa; James manages the gallery, while his wife Emma is a wildlife artist. Both of them know the wildlife of Africa very well – they've built their lives around it, and both James and Emma have built a business selling Emma's wildlife paintings. He told me a story about his sales pitch to a man who walked into their gallery one day. James told the man about how they had seen the lion in the painting in its natural habitat in Kenya. James enthused about this amazing animal and expected that the customer would appreciate this story, because most of their customers shared their passion for Africa's animals. But in this case it was different. James told me with some embarrassment that, after talking about the lion for some time, the client said that he had no interest whatsoever in wildlife. He was considering buying a painting because of its investment value. James changed tack. He spoke about the credentials of his artist wife, the sales they had made through various galleries internationally, and some of their more esteemed clients. Now he started selling the painting as an investment, rather than a treasured possession of a wildlife enthusiast.

James had failed to listen first. He was barking up the wrong tree, and assumed he knew what the customer wanted, but he got it wrong. He reflected that instead of launching into a sales pitch, he should listen more – even though he'd managed to change tack and rescue the sale, he should have begun with some open questions. Then he has the chance to understand the potential client's perspectives and their needs. Listening is a crucial part of selling.

Key Points

Listening is a crucial part of selling. We need to find out about customers' needs. Don't make assumptions.

What to do next

- Make a point of listening to customers and asking questions, so as to find out what they really value. Don't make assumptions. Ask open questions to get them talking first.

- Resolve that next time you talk with a customer, ask them about their needs first.

See also...

40 Why awards don't matter

Tobias is one of the directors of a large graphic design company
in Sweden that has won a number of industry awards. He and his
colleagues were proud of these awards and rightly so. At one of
my workshops he told me that they always featured these awards
in their marketing communications. However, one day a customer
asked Tobias: 'So what?' In other words, the customer was asking:
'What good is that to me?' Tobias said that for a moment he was
flummoxed, wrong-footed by this question. For Tobias it seemed
obvious that winning awards was good – it proved they had the
respect of the industry, and were good at their chosen profession.
But that perspective was being challenged and Tobias had to answer
the question from the customer's point of view.

The answer was easy.

They had won the award in question because their packaging design
had increased sales for a manufacturing client and allowed them
to increase the price of the newly-packaged product. Aha! Now the
customer was interested. Now the customer wanted to talk about
how their graphic design skills and advertising expertise could be
used to help him to increase his own sales, prices and profits. (And
if the company won an award for it, fine, but frankly the customer
didn't care about that.)

The point is that winning an award is not a customer benefit. It is the
design work that helped the client's profitability that was a customer
benefit. In emphasising prizes and awards, Tobias' company was
talking about what was in it for them, not what was in it for the
customer. The trap of talking about features – not benefits – had
taken another victim.

Looking at it from the outside, it's easy to see where they went
wrong. As outsiders, it's easy to give advice (that's what I do as a
consultant!) But before looking down on the mistakes of others, look
at yourself. We're all guilty of falling into this trap to some extent, so
spend some time looking at your own marketing messages and use

the 'So What?' test to ruthlessly examine every nook and cranny of your marketing communications for evidence of this error.

Key Points

Some things matter much more to us than to customers. Identify these things and de-prioritise them in marketing communications. Highlight instead what **does** matter to customers.

What to do next

- Examine your own marketing communications. Are you talking about customer benefits or what matters to you?

- Ask a colleague or an outsider to scrutinize your marketing communications to identify customer benefits and weed out anything that does not convey benefits.

See also...

51 What are they buying from you really?   *145*

41 Why my website didn't get any hits

In my marketing consultancy and training work, I advise design, media and technology businesses about the danger of failing to emphasise benefits. So I'm embarrassed to admit that I've fallen into the same trap myself.

Some years ago, a revised version of my website highlighted my academic and professional qualifications. Before it went live I decided to do what I always advise clients to do – that is, to ask customers. I called a couple of ex-clients, with whom I'd kept in touch and whose opinions I trusted, to ask them what they thought of my new website. Both of them said the same thing. They each said that my academic qualifications were not the point, that they were not the reason they'd engaged me as a consultant in the first place, nor the reason they recommended me to other people. Instead, both of them said that the main benefit to customers was my style of working, which allowed customers to think things through in their own terms, the way that I worked within the context of their business, and how I helped them to find appropriate solutions.

By featuring my academic qualifications, I was emphasising features but not benefits – facts about myself rather than results for the customer. Even worse, you might say that to some extent the website had been designed for me and not for them; it talked about what I wanted to say, not what they needed to know. Whoops!

Years later, I tripped again with this same 'features not benefits' problem.

Having published a new version of my website I sent out personalised emails in small batches to my contacts with the message: 'David Parrish has a new website'. This resulted in almost no hits, so I sent the next batch of emails with the message using capital letters: 'DAVID PARRISH HAS A NEW WEBSITE!!' I still didn't get the traffic I expected. At this point, confused, I stopped. I decided to have a word with myself. Metaphorically, I tapped myself on the shoulder and beckoned myself to take my consultant's advice.

What would I say to a client at this point?

I would say that they're making the mistake of communicating features and not benefits. The fact that David Parrish has a new website is a feature, but customers' response could easily be 'So what?' Anybody receiving the email could say, 'OK, good for you!' – and then delete it. In fact, that's what I do with many email newsletters ('News from XYZ company'). So I stopped, and had a think. I looked at the emails from the customer's point of view. Then I changed the subject line to 'Cool business ideas for creative entrepreneurs like you!' And then there was a response. I received hits on my website, and the traffic increased.

Why?

Because at last I was communicating what was in it for the customer. Finally, I was telling them what they could get out of it, rather than what I put into it. The message had been turned around to say what was in it for them. At last I was talking about benefits, not features.

I'm embarrassed to admit this, especially as a marketing consultant, but these stories only go to show how difficult it is to step outside our own business when we're enthusiastic about it and want to promote it. Instead of jumping around with excitement, we need to coolly examine what we are offering in terms of customer benefits and talk in the customers' language, not our own.

Key Points

It's easy to fall into the trap of talking about our business from our own perspective (features) rather than saying what's in it for the customer (benefits).

What to do next

- Ensure your communications present benefits for customers, rather than irrelevant facts of interest only to you.

- Test all marketing communications in this way before publishing them, writing down on a simple evaluation sheet the customer benefit you are expressing.

See also...

51 What are they buying from you really?   *145*

By changing our perspective towards the customers' point of view, we get into the good habit of challenging our own assumptions about what customers want.

We learn what customers really value by asking open questions and then listening.

This leads us nicely into talking about the things that *they* value in our marketing communications.

At the same time, let's remember in communicating with them that these customers are real people...

PART EIGHT

It's personal

Why customers need to know, like and trust you

Word of mouth marketing is cost effective and can work brilliantly. This is despite some people's view that it doesn't count as 'proper marketing'.

If you deliver a personal service, then personality matters as much as competence. The more that customers need to know, like and trust you, the more important it is that your marketing communications show your people and their personalities. Customers don't want to buy personal services from faceless companies.

Clients tend to stay with businesses they know, like and trust. This factor can override matters of pricing and the superior competence of rivals. Customers stick to the 'devil they know'. That is, until they are upset personally.

42 It's not 'proper marketing'

Pedro, an entrepreneur in Colombia, told me he wasn't able to do any real marketing because of a lack of budget in the early stage of his web design business. He assured me that once he had generated some profits he would devise 'a proper marketing plan'. No problem, I said – I understand the situation, especially at an early stage of a business, when money is tight. But I also said to him that he **had** managed to win clients over the last several months and delivered several successful projects.

I asked him how those projects came about and where he found the clients. He told me, very apologetically, that they had been simply word-of-mouth recommendations. The first website was for an ex-colleague who heard he was going into business and happened to need a website. Soon afterwards, this client recommended him to a business associate and Pedro won another contract. And so it went on, from customer to customer. It intrigued me that Pedro was so apologetic about winning clients in this way without ever advertising, without what he would call 'a proper marketing plan'.

On the other hand, I remember a client who had set up in business using a redundancy payment after losing his day job. He spent £5,000 on advertising and attracted no new customers at all. The whole amount was wasted. And he had what he thought was 'a proper marketing plan.'

Word-of-mouth is the oldest promotional technique in the world. From the moment human beings learned to communicate they were advising others about what to do, where to go, and what to buy. So why is word-of-mouth regarded as 'not proper marketing'? Why is word-of-mouth marketing disparaged in this way?

Personally, I think that it's the best kind of marketing communication – certainly the cheapest, and one of the most effective. In the digital era, it can be even more powerful. Video testimonials are inexpensive to produce. Customers talk to each other electronically, globally and rapidly using social media. Word of mouth promotion is more powerful than ever before.

Key Points

Word of mouth marketing is cost effective and can work brilliantly. This is despite some people's view that it doesn't count as 'proper marketing'.

What to do next

- Encourage your customers to tell friends and colleagues about your business by word of mouth, both in person and online.

- Contact your top five customers and politely ask them (perhaps over lunch or a drink) to recommend you to their colleagues and contacts.

See also...

43 Who the Hell is 'info'?

As a management consultant I advised an advertising company in Scotland. Before my first visit I looked at their website and saw that they had a wonderful portfolio of work and an interesting list of clients. However, I didn't get a sense of how big the company was, how many employees they had, or whether they were younger or older people. It was an impersonal website, even though it was stylish, with an intriguing, but abstract, business name.

I was welcomed into the office by two young women, the owners. In conversation I mentioned that, looking at their website, I had no idea that this company was owned and managed by two young women, which was quite unusual. (I emphasise that I was not making any value judgements here, simply stating a fact.) They explained that they'd deliberately hidden their gender and age, since they found that many potential clients had a prejudice against young women. I said that surely the customer would find out at some point that they were in fact two young women. If some customers really felt that they couldn't trust the competence of young women, then they would not get their business anyway. On the other hand, for customers who might actually **prefer** to do work with young women, there was no way they could find out. In short, they would 'get found out' at some point, so why not simply come clean and publish the truth about themselves? This would simply save everybody's time and quicken the process that would happen anyway, deterring some potential customers but at the same time attracting others.

I've found countless examples of businesses in the creative and digital sector whose websites don't allow you to assess the actual people involved in delivering the services. These websites emphasise competence and professionalism. They may even have a show reel, a list of clients, and testimonials. But they actually **hide their people**!

Don't hide your people![13] is the title of a blog I wrote about this. It was a rant against the impersonal website which ostensibly

---

13 http://blog.davidparrish.com/tshirts_and_suits/2009/12/dont-hide-your-people.html

advertises a friendly company, yet refuses to show who is involved within it. These websites often say 'give us a ring for a chat', or 'call around for a cup of coffee'. Then they invite you to get in touch using an online form. They expect you to give details including your name, email address (and sometimes I wonder if next they're going to ask us for a blood sample). Yet they don't have the courtesy to display their own names! It really annoys me when they say 'contact info@[companyname].com' or email 'hello@[companyname].com'.

I don't want to do business with somebody called 'info'! Why aren't they prepared to give me their name? Why not say 'ring John Smith' or 'email Amy Brown'? Why are they hiding? What have they got to hide? Are they not really human beings? Are they Martians? Is the company actually run by dogs? Or robots? Call me old-fashioned if you like, but I want to know the name of the person I'm going to be speaking to. I want to get a sense of the human beings inside the organisation. Is that too much to expect?

These businesses expect potential customers to 'get naked' in front of them and yet they themselves are hiding behind the door. Their websites are like concrete walls with a small slit for you to post your requirements. There's no shop window where you can look inside to see who's there. This approach is the complete antithesis of being customer friendly.

If we want people to actually know, trust and like us, we need to come out and show our personalities. Is it too much to expect a photograph of the owner and staff on the website, together with some information about them? Many websites do this of course. What I find staggering is the number that don't.

The owners of these impersonal websites misunderstand customers' needs. They think the customer simply needs to know about their competence. But competence, though necessary, is not sufficient. The customer also is wondering 'Can I deal with these people?', 'Can I trust them?', 'What are they **like**?' It's this second element that is often missing.

'Your differences is your strength' is the motto of an artist friend of mine, when giving business advice. That motto came to mind at this time. By being our authentic selves, by not equivocating or hiding, we simultaneously deter some customers and attract others. Yes, we will 'lose' some potential business, but we would never win that business anyway. On the other hand, those customers who love what we actually are will be all the more attracted to us, and more quickly.

So don't hide your people. Of course you may have reason to hide, if you think that customers won't like you! The truth is, some will like you and some won't. So let's just get on with it, tell them about ourselves. This will deter some people but attract others. This will happen anyway and the sooner we put our cards on the table, the sooner we will connect with the right kind of customers. By **not** hiding, you will allow people to know, like and trust you.

Show your personalities as well as your competencies in your marketing communications.

Key Points

The more that customers need to know, like and trust you, the more important it is that your marketing communications show your people and personalities. People don't want to buy personal services from faceless companies. Don't hide your people; come out! This will deter some customers but attract others – the right ones.

What to do next

- Ask someone who doesn't already know your business (eg a friend of a friend) what they can tell from your marketing communications about the people in your business.

- Emphasise not only competence in your marketing communications, but also your personality.

- Always invite potential customers to contact a real person, with a real name. Adding a photo of that person is even better.

See also...

44 Follow the love

When I was small, my mum told me: 'It's not what you know, it's **who** you know that matters'. In my early 20s I founded a business and, of course, undertook some advertising and promotional activity. Later, I managed other businesses including an international book distribution and marketing company. Then I went to business school, read lots of marketing books and was enchanted by complex marketing strategies and theories. Some of them I put into practice. Now, many years later, I've come full circle, back to the conclusion that in many respects, it's not what you know, but who you know that matters.

Despite all the fancy marketing communications techniques, business is fundamentally about the connection between **people**. Corporations don't do business and brands don't do business. It's **people** that do business.

In order to do business with you, people need to know, like and trust you. Of course, the degree to which this is true varies with the type of business. For a completely impersonal business, perhaps one in which the transactions are online without any personal communication whatsoever, then it doesn't matter. However, if some kind of personal relationship is needed to deliver the product, it **does** matter. And so this applies to the vast majority of services, and also to products where the customer is in some way involved. It matters greatly if the transaction involves personal communication with the client.

If your business is in any way personal, it needs customers to know, like and trust you. This is best conveyed by other customers who recommend you by word-of-mouth, or testimonials, or by other means. In these circumstances, your most valuable promotional asset is your customer base, the people who already know you, like and trust you – and have actually seen you deliver the goods. These people can authentically advertise how good you are, in a much more believable way than anything we could ever say about ourselves.

Use these relationships.

Actually ask customers to recommend you. Reward them as appropriate. This could be a matter of offering them a commission on new work they recommend, but sometimes this isn't necessary, and could even be counter-productive. Usually, a sincere thank you or a small gift for helping you win a new customer is all that is required to repay the favour and encourage further recommendations.

In discussing this issue with one of my consultancy clients, in which I emphasised the need to use satisfied customers to win new business, Stella said, 'So David, what you're saying is "follow the love"?' Actually, that's not the way I would have expressed it, but she was absolutely right.

Follow the love!

Key Points

It's all about people, really. People need to know, like and trust you if your business relates to customers in a personal way. Happy customers can lead you to new customers.

What to do next

- Use the relationship you have with customers who love you. Follow the love.

- Ask happy customers to recommend you to other potential customers.

See also...

55 Maybe you're the brand   *154*

45 Do Google rankings matter?

Search engine optimisation (SEO) specialists will sell you a service of using keywords, meta data, and other clever techniques to ensure that your website is listed high in Google's rankings. The question to ask yourself is – to what extent customers actually choose you as a supplier because they find you easily on Google?

For some businesses, a high Google ranking will do the trick; for other businesses it's almost irrelevant. And this relevance relates to the degree of personal trust required. If I were selling stationery, I would definitely want to be listed high on Google rankings for stationery. But for more personal businesses I don't think it's quite so important, because customers also need to know whether or not they can trust you, and they need to find this out somehow. And they will more likely find out from word of mouth than from your website.

If I needed to find a supplier I could actually trust, I would be prepared to scroll down Google rankings until I found something that convinced me – perhaps a video, customer testimonials, or other evidence. And so I think that Google rankings are important in direct proportion to the degree to which the businesses is totally impersonal.

Customer testimonials can help tremendously.

We can say we're wonderful until we're blue in the face, but it just doesn't count. We would say that, wouldn't we? But when somebody else says it, it's much more believable. Customer testimonials in writing or on video are very valuable. When customers compliment us on a job well done, ask them if they'd be willing to put their comments in writing. Ask them immediately; strike while the iron is hot. Email them with a suggested statement, inviting them to edit it if required, and requesting they confirm by returning an email in agreement. This makes it easy for them to do. A bonus is that the **process** of asking past customers for testimonials provides additional opportunities. By contacting past customers we can win repeat business or undertake authentic market research. We might encourage them to recommend us to other people.

Before investing in search engine optimisation services, ask yourself, to what extent customers are likely to choose your business and products purely from Google rankings? The more personal your business, the less likely it is to be so.

Key Points

Google rankings matter more for some businesses than others. For impersonal businesses, Google ranking is more likely to be a major factor; for personal businesses it's less so.

What to do next

- Review recent approaches from potential customers and measure the percentage that contacted you because of a Google search. This helps you assess the degree of importance of SEO to your business.

- Take into account the degree to which customers need to trust you personally when considering how much to invest in SEO.

See also...

46 Observe yourself

We need to be able to look at things from the customers' point of view. This is actually quite difficult to do. Nevertheless, we must still try. We have certain assumptions about customers' needs. We expect customers to behave in a way that suits us.

A useful exercise is to actually watch yourself when you're on the other side of the fence, when you are a consumer. Watch yourself and ask yourself, how do you actually choose suppliers?

For me, if I need some stationery, I simply select a company online that offers the right price and delivery. I don't need to know about the personalities involved. But if I need a photographer to come into my house, then I need to know two things. Firstly, whether or not they're competent and qualified. Secondly, whether I trust them to do a good job without letting me down or ripping me off. The first element is easy to ascertain. I can look at their photos and credentials such as membership of a professional association. The second element is much more difficult and I find myself faced with a choice of scores of available photographers near my home. I don't know how to choose between them, so, in practice I ring a friend and ask if they can recommend somebody.

Is your business one where customers simply do not care about the people involved? Or is it a business where a customer is likely to be concerned about who will actually be doing the job?

If it's the latter, then no end of competence or qualifications will be sufficient to persuade them – they also need to know about you and your people. Word-of-mouth recommendation is best. We can also introduce ourselves with a video and win over the confidence of potential customers using customer testimonials.

So I say that there are different kinds of businesses: absolutely non-personal at one end of the spectrum, and ultra personal at the other. And of course all grades in between the two extremes. We need to decide where we are on that scale and the level of personal trust needed by the customer in order to do business with us, before we decide on our marketing communications.

Key Points

Consumers behave in ways we don't always expect or understand. Gain insights into customer behavior by observing yourself when you are a consumer.

What to do next

• Observe your behaviour as a consumer. What makes you decide to buy one product rather than another? What do you expect from businesses that try to sell things to you? How important to you are the actual people involved when buying different kinds of products?

See also...

47 Analyse successes as well as failures

Analyse your failures. If you fail to win a pitch, for example, you'll probably undertake some kind of post-mortem. Where did it go wrong? What can you do about it? What will you do next time? But when we win, we tend **not** to analyse things half as thoroughly. We should undertake a post-mortem here too, and ask **why** we were successful. Investigate the real reason we won the contract in the face of stiff competition. This might lead to insights about our competitive advantage.

Let's face it, more than half of it was probably because we already had an existing relationship with the client. Let's not assume that we were the most competent. The frightening thing is, the competition was probably better than us in terms of ability, but we hung on to the contract because of the relationship. Let's celebrate the relationship, but let's not get complacent about the need to constantly improve our competence too.

So, if personal relationships matter that much, let's capitalise on them. Let's go through our address books and contact past customers. Let's consolidate relationships with our existing clients and take them out for lunch. Let's strengthen the bonds. Let's encourage them to use word-of-mouth to tell other people about how good we are. Not only how competent we are, but also what fun we are to work with.

Key Points

We can learn not only from failures but successes. It's important that we fully understand the reasons for our successes. It may be more to do with relationships than skills.

What to do next

- Review your address book and capitalise on relationships you have with current and past customers.

- Find five past customers and speak with them, perhaps over lunch or a drink.

See also...

48 Trust trumps competence

People tend to stick with the same suppliers. Research shows that people are more likely to change their marriage partner than their bank. There's an inertia that works against changing suppliers. However, what research also shows is that the trigger for change is usually something personal. In most cases, customers change suppliers not because of price or service, but because they've been in some way offended or upset by another human being. This could be an unfriendly delivery driver or a rude receptionist. This, for me, shows how very personal business is. (They also say that the doctors who actually get sued by patients are not the ones who make the most horrendous mistakes, but the ones who fail to apologise sincerely. It seems that a surgeon can cut off the wrong leg and still not be sued, provided that they apologise properly, whereas a doctor who removes the wrong toenail but is then dismissive of the patient's complaint will soon find themselves in court.)

Yes, personal relationships matter.

Customers would rather have 'the devil they know' than the devil they don't know. They tend to stick with the same suppliers. This can be extremely frustrating if you are on the outside trying to get in. Every month I hear a complaint from some business owner who has pitched for a job, only to find that the client has re-engaged their previous supplier. The incumbent won the new contract. It can be frustrating and sometimes there's a sense that it was a 'done deal', and that the time invested by other would-be suppliers was wasted. For me, I think it shows that all other things being equal, the customer would rather work with a supplier whom they already know, like, trust and have actually seen deliver. I would go further and say that even if things are **not** equal – even if the new kids on the block are actually more competent than their current suppliers – the customer would still rather stay with the supplier with whom they have an established personal relationship.

This demonstrates that competence is necessary but not sufficient.

Competence is only half the story. The other half is the relationship. And to win work we need both. Additional competence does not compensate for lack of trust. Some technology companies are staffed by people who are brilliant programmers but lack the social skills to establish a personal rapport with customers. This imbalance doesn't work. An abundance of qualifications, competence, and track record does not compensate for any perceived gap in the customer's faith that you can deliver and that they can work with you effectively.

Yes, my clients complain when they've tried to win a new customer, only to be defeated by the incumbent supplier. Funnily enough, they never complain (or suggest that it's bordering on corruption) when they themselves are the incumbent supplier. They never complain when they're reappointed by a customer who's seen them deliver successfully, and for whom they're a known quantity.

Customers need to trust you personally as well as have confidence in your competence. In the end, trust trumps competence.

Key Points

Clients tend to stay with businesses they know, like and trust. This factor can override matters of pricing and even the superior competence of rivals. Customers stick to the 'devil they know'. That is, until customers are upset personally.

What to do next

- Recognise that it may be difficult to dislodge a potential client from their regular supplier. At the same time, appreciate the advantage you have as a supplier to your own clients. Focus on keeping your customers.

See also...

In many ways, marketing is simple – if only we remember that it's all about real people.

People like to work with people they like; people need to trust their suppliers; people relate to others on a human level. People will talk to their friends about you.

Base your marketing on how real people actually behave – and how they see things.

Explore what your customers mean when they talk about 'quality'…

PART NINE

What customers see is not what you see

Understanding customers' perspectives

We need to look at our businesses from the outside, from the customers' point of view. This is very difficult to do, so we need to ask customers how **they** see things. Quality is not objective – it's subjective. Quality is fitness for purpose. And ultimately it's the customer who decides how quality is defined. Failure to look at things from the customers' point of view can be costly, especially when other cultures or languages are involved.

Business names are for customers, not the business owners. Don't choose a name customers won't understand, are unable to pronounce or don't know how to spell. Choose a name for your business that works for customers. Despite your company name, customers might recommend you personally. Maybe you are the brand really.

49 Customers' eyes

'O would some power the gift to give us to see ourselves as others see us,' wrote Scottish poet Robert Burns.

If only we could see our businesses through customers' eyes!

One of the most important things to do in marketing is to look at our business through the eyes of customers. Looking at things from the customers' point of view is at the heart of marketing. But it's extremely difficult, because we're inside the business, not outside of it, as customers are. We know the business in all its details: in some ways, we know too much. And this makes it very difficult to look at things as customers do, from the outside. Yet it's what we must do.

Ask customers how they see our business. Finding opportunities to listen to customers by using questionnaires, feedback mechanisms or simply asking them face-to-face helps us see our own businesses through customers' eyes.

Key Points

Try to look afresh at your business from the outside. This is very difficult to do, so ask customers.

What to do next

- Get fresh insights about your business by asking customers – and non-customers.

- Ask five relevant people this month for their opinions about your enterprise.

See also...

50 Quality, yes. But whose quality?

At one stage I was a consultant to a Braille library, a charity that transcribed books into Braille, to be lent to blind people. One reader complained that it took more than three months for a book to be available in Braille after it had been published in paperback – he wanted to read a book at the same time as his sighted wife was reading the paperback. And so he asked for a quick version to be made available. The library refused because quality was paramount – they didn't want to sully their excellent reputation by releasing a book that was imperfect. Given that it took several weeks to produce a Braille book, the reader would simply have to wait. In response, the reader said that, for him, **time** was a quality issue. He said he would prefer to have an imperfect copy with some typographical errors at a much earlier stage, than wait for a perfect copy that was of much less use in terms of his simultaneous enjoyment of the book with his wife. In the end, the library decided to offer two versions of Braille books, including imperfect first editions, so that readers could choose.

Quality is a matter for the customer to decide, not the producer.

So what is quality? One definition is that quality is 'fitness for purpose'. Using this definition, we're forced to look at things from the customer's point of view. And so a plastic fork, given away free with a take-away meal is perfectly suited to its purpose and so in the circumstances is of higher quality than an expensive piece of silver cutlery. The video camera bundled with a smart phone is in some ways of higher quality than a broadcast standard camera if we take into account its availability, accessibility and ease-of-use. The grainy footage from a mobile phone shown on TV news is better quality than the professional TV camera that wasn't at the scene.

A filmmaking company told me that their real expertise was in making long documentary films of a high quality. But some customers wanted a film with a much smaller budget. They said that they couldn't compromise on quality and were therefore turning away such business. This provoked a discussion about the definition of 'quality'. Surely, I said, a short film could be produced with the same level of quality, for a smaller budget? A short film could be produced economically by limiting the number of locations used, careful planning, and specifying the project within certain parameters. After some discussion they agreed. They now make short films that satisfy customers' need for quality on a budget. These films also satisfy the criteria of quality from their own point of view as professional filmmakers.

In discussing matters of quality, we need to first of all decide whose definition of quality is more important. Yours, or the customers'?

Key Points

Quality is not objective, it's subjective. Quality is fitness for purpose. Ultimately it's the customer who decides how quality is defined.

What to do next

- Avoid falling into the trap of defining quality only from the producer's point of view. Ask customers about their view of quality. Theirs is the definition that matters most.

- Organise a focus group of customers to ask them about the qualities they most value in your products.

See also...

51 What are they buying from you really?

I gave business advice to a theatre company that delivers drama
projects with communities, often sponsored by local authorities.
Their theatre projects are carefully designed to ensure artistic
quality. They pride themselves on the quality of their work in artistic
terms. But on reflection, they recognise that they win these contracts
for different reasons. In reality, it's not only because of the quality
of their theatre work, but because of their success in engaging
communities. They engage with marginalised communities and
disenfranchised young people, who are notoriously difficult to
work with. Yet the company has the ability to engage and inspire
them through theatre projects. **That's** their speciality, and that's
what the customer really wants. And the paying customer is the
local authority. This is why they are selected over and above their
rivals. Moreover they can provide evidence the local authority
needs to back up this community engagement. At first they thought
the paperwork was just a necessary inconvenience, but now
they recognise it's actually at the heart of what they're selling to
the customer.

What are **you** selling really? Or, looking at it from the customer's
point of view, what is the customer buying **really**? This sounds like
a silly question, because there's always an obvious answer – a 'first-
level answer'. It's the product that's stated on the invoice. But
things are often much more complex than that because, alongside
the main transaction, there are unstated extras. There may be an
experience, or perhaps a feel-good factor. Perhaps there's some
social status involved in the transaction. Or there are social benefits
in working with the people involved.

We all know that the Harley-Davidson company sells motorbikes.
But this is an example of what I call a 'first-level answer'. So what
are they selling **really**? An executive from the Harley-Davidson
company was quoted as saying this: *'What we sell is the ability
for a 43-year-old accountant to dress in black leather, ride through
small towns, and have people be afraid of him.'* In other words,
they're selling a solution to a mid-life crisis. They sell the weekend

145

experience of pretending to be a Hell's Angel. You might say they are selling not so much a feel-good factor as a 'feel-bad' factor.

Hong Kong designer fashion company Dialog undertook a charity project to make t-shirts and donated the profits to victims of a natural disaster. They called these t-shirts 'Hope Tees' because the project brought hope to the communities benefiting from the profits generated. They packaged the t-shirts with a printed card telling the story of the project. Later, after carrying out some informal market research, they found that many people who had bought the t-shirts hadn't worn them, or even opened the package. The company was intrigued and asked further questions. They discovered that people were buying t-shirts to support the project, not as an item of clothing to wear themselves. In reality, customers weren't buying t-shirts – they were buying hope. So the article I wrote about this is entitled *'Selling hope, wrapped up in t-shirts'*[14].

We all need crucial insights into what the customer actually wants to buy. We have to discover what customers define as quality and what they truly value. In short, we need fully to understand customers' perspectives. We need to gain a clear understanding of what matters to customers. To do this we need to listen to customers.

Key Points

What the customer is really buying from you may be different from what you think you are selling.

What to do next

- Look beneath the surface and understand what customers are really buying from you.

- Engage an outsider to ask your customers what they really value about your product.

---

14 www.tss-ideasinaction.com

See also...

52 How to reverse the advertising message

An advertisement for washing powder simply had three images: dirty washing, a washing machine using the detergent advertised, and then clean washing. It was a very simple and effective concept. The only problem was that this was published in a Middle Eastern country, where Arabic readers read from right to left. The failure to look at things through the eyes of an Arabic reader reversed the message. This is because it was designed by Europeans who assumed that everyone reads from left to right. To me, this reveals a disdainful lack of interest in the culture of the target audience.

There are many examples of mistakes that have been made as a result of a business not looking at things from the customer's point of view. Misunderstanding other cultures and languages creates many problems.

An American company was going to launch a new brand of beer in the UK and call this golden beverage Ambrosia. After all, Ambrosia is the name of the nectar of the gods. A perfect name you might think, except for one thing. In the UK the word Ambrosia is also a well-known brand of tinned rice pudding. In the UK most people have eaten Ambrosia rice pudding. It is deeply ingrained in the minds of UK customers that Ambrosia means rice pudding. Luckily, the American chief executive had a British deputy who told him of this cultural phenomenon, and the brand name was changed just in time.

It can be fatal to **assume** that we know the customer. We probably don't know what the customer thinks about a brand name, how they define quality, or how people read. In all these examples the solution is simple. We should actually ask them. To ask one Arabic reader what he thought of the washing powder advert would have taken very little money. Money wasn't the issue; attitude was the problem. The barrier to this simple market research was not budget, but arrogance. What we need is the right attitude. We need to adopt a mindset that customers might know something we don't know.

Key Points

Failure to look at things from the customers' point of view can be costly. This is especially the case when other cultures or languages are involved.

What to do next

- Take care to test advertisements with actual users. If other languages or cultures are involved, make sure you consult with a native speaker or member of the target community. Make this part of your business system.

- Make it company policy to test all communications first with real customers.

See also...

53 The foreigner's advantage

I sometimes find that I'm more valued overseas than in my own country. Overseas, I'm a novelty. Abroad, I'm out of the ordinary. Ironically, I'm not regarded as an 'international speaker' in England. Yet foreigners fly me across the world to speak at their conferences in China, Sweden, Chile, Russia and Korea.

Of course, doing business overseas has its complications. But it can also have massive advantages. Sometimes the foreign is more attractive. In a different setting, the ordinary becomes exotic. Foreign products can be cool.

This is what I call the 'foreigner's advantage'.

Foreignness can be a benefit in certain circumstances. Play to your strengths. Or to put it another way, deploy your characteristics where they become strengths. Your local ordinariness may be exotic abroad.

Key Points

Sometimes, the very fact that a product is foreign makes it attractive. Maybe you and your products are more appealing outside your own country.

What to do next

- Find ways of finding out how customers in other countries might value your products.

- Get out a map and make a list of territories in your own country or abroad where your products might have particular appeal.

See also...

54 Your business name is not for you

Your business name is for your customers, not for you. I'm dismayed by a trading name if I don't understand it, I'm unsure about how it's spelled, or I can't pronounce it. Sometimes, when I ask the business owners, the name turn out to be private jokes between themselves, or a reference to a personal experience, or in-house jargon that's meaningful only to the people within the business. Some business names are alienating and confusing to people outside the business – including customers!

We've all experienced an uncomfortable situation when we don't understand a private joke, or when there's something going on in a social situation that we don't understand. That's exactly how customers feel when they don't 'get it'; when the name of a business doesn't make sense to them. If you want to make customers feel awkward, or totally alienate them, choose a name for your business that works for you – but not for them.

If you spend just a microsecond considering a business name not from your own point of view, but from the point of view of customers, we'd never make such a big mistake. For me, names are not so much an indication of the lack of intelligence of the business owners, but their attitude that the business is fundamentally for them and about them – not for and about customers. And that makes my heart sink on behalf of the business owners. If they have such disregard for customers, their business is likely to fail.

A brand is much more than your trading name and/or logo. A brand conveys a promise to customers and a consistent message delivered to them in every way. A brand includes how you interact with your customers at each and every touchpoint. It's the 'personality' of your business, its language and tone of voice. It encompasses everything from how the phone is answered to how deliveries are wrapped.

A focused marketing strategy will help you develop a brand that works for customers. Customers need to understand clearly what the business represents. Consequently the fewer products, or the more closely related a range of products, the more likely the customer will understand what you're about. We don't see too many businesses in the creative and digital industries that confuse customers by offering an unintegrated range of products or services, simply because those businesses don't last very long. On the other hand, the most enduring brands are absolutely clear about their expertise, their place in a competitive market, what they do and they don't do, and the key messages they want to convey to their chosen customers.

In the tale of 'Julie the Jeweller' (see section *57 The 3Ms of marketing*), we recognise that from the point of view of customers, Julie actually has two businesses. Looking at each of her target markets and considering the keywords at the heart of the marketing messages for each, her two markets may require different brands. On the one hand, the messages were about elegance, exclusivity and expense, and on the other hand the messages were about colour, fun and coolness. It's easy to see that the most appropriate brand for each audience, based on different messages, will be very different.

Key Points

Business names are for customers, not the business owners. Don't choose a name customers won't understand, be unable to pronounce or won't know how to spell. Choose a name that works for customers.

What to do next

- Ask your customers what they think of your trading name. Even better, ask non-customers what kind of business they think your name represents. Consider changing your business name. Or, as first aid, adopt an explanatory strapline.

- Make a list of five customers and five non-customers (including target clients and ex-customers). Ask all ten of them to comment on your brand.

See also...

55 Maybe you're the brand

For small businesses, the **person** is often the brand in reality. Since a brand is more than a name and includes all the messages and behaviours of a business, it can be personified in the business owner. For many small businesses, despite their official name, customers talk about the owner. Irrespective of what their website says, customers observe the behaviour of the owner. For a corporation with a large number of people, each employee represents the brand to some extent, but none is in the spotlight as much as the owner of a small business. In contrast, for one-person businesses and small companies, the owner personifies the brand. Then, customers will often refer to the business by the name of the owner, not its trading name. For example, when clients want to find a publisher I recommend Fiona Shaw, not her company, Wordscapes Ltd.

The key is to look at things from the customer's point of view.

What are customers telling other people?

What's the word on the street?

Are they talking about your business using its official name, or the name of the central person involved?

The customer is king. If everyone out there is talking about Fiona Shaw, then perhaps we should go with this, rather than try to impose a trading name when people want to use a personal name. That's not to say there is no benefit in having a trading name and a logo. At the same time, to encourage word-of-mouth promotion, we need to recognise the language customers prefer to use. If that language is about people rather than the company's name, it indicates that the personal relationship is of prime importance for the customer. And if people want to talk about **you** rather than your company, then we need to at least make sure that you are prominently featured on your company's website. If that's what they want to do, let customers focus on you rather than the brand.

Listen to what customers are saying. Are they talking to each other about the company name or the key person?

Key Points

Despite your company name, customers might recommend you. Maybe **you** are the brand really.

What to do next

- Find out what the word is on the street. If people are talking about you rather than your company name, make sure you are featured prominently in marketing communications.

- In a quick survey, ask ten customers whether recommendations (to them or from them) used the company name or the name of the key individual in the business.

See also...

It's fascinating to step outside our own way of thinking and get into the minds of customers.

Understanding what customers mean by quality, and how they talk about your business is not only interesting – it's commercially valuable.

Knowing this stuff helps us to craft precise messages to them...

PART TEN

Communicating with precision
Who should say what to whom, and how

There are probably several distinct markets or 'audiences' for your business and each needs to hear a different message, appropriate to their own needs. The 3Ms technique forces us to think through marketing communications in the right order: **Market**, then **Message**, and then **Medium**. The pros and cons of any medium can only be evaluated in the context of the business objectives, prioritisation of markets and key messages.

Customers talk with each other like never before. Word of mouth is electronic, rapid and global. Advertisers no longer control the message; customers do. All we can do is be open and give them stories to tell. Listening is a key part of selling. By listening you can address the customer's needs and wants more precisely.

Strategic marketing is a top-level responsibility and so the chief executive is the chief marketing officer. It's not easy but it's got to be done. In the end, that's what chief executives are paid for.

56 Different markets

Stan's Café is a performance group based in Birmingham UK and an enterprise I featured in my Creative, Cultural and Digital Industries Guide[15]. The directors at Stan's Café recognise that they have three distinct types of customers.

1. Audiences: the people who actually put their 'bums on seats' and pay for tickets

2. Venues and promoters: the organisations that host their work and help to promote it to audiences

3. Sponsors, stakeholders and other supporters

Each audience has different interests and needs to know different things, so by clarifying the distinction between these different audiences, Stan's Café recognises that they need to convey different messages to each of them. Then, the media they use to communicate has to be appropriate to each particular audience and message.

Precision marketing helps us to identify the different markets for any particular product and how we can best communicate effectively to each specific market. For any one product, there are often several distinct markets.

Of course, much of this we do instinctively anyway, without using any particular technique. We know that we need to speak to venues in a different way than to audiences. We know that communication to key stakeholders needs to be different than promotional materials produced for audiences. However, the benefit of being more methodical is that we don't miss any opportunities, we don't get our wires crossed, and we don't compromise or water-down our communications. In this way, all marketing communications are clear, appropriate and precise.

Key Points

There are probably several distinct markets or 'audiences' for your business and each needs to hear a different message, appropriate to their own needs.

What to do next

• Identify different types of 'audiences' relevant to your business. Then decide the key messages for each audience. Then choose the most useful medium to communicate with them.

See also...

57 The 3Ms of marketing

Julie, a jeweller, asked me for some marketing advice. With a limited budget for marketing communications, she couldn't decide whether to invest in a better website or in a printed brochure to promote her products. She asked my advice about this dilemma. In my workshops I ask the question that Julie asked me. Some people argue in favour of a website, saying that it's more versatile and can be updated more frequently with new products or prices. Others argue in favour of a printed brochure, because it can more accurately illustrate the jewellery on sale. In other words, a discussion ensues and we take a vote.

The problem is that Julie's question was the **wrong question**.

Julie's question focused on the medium, not the message or the market segments. Sometimes a management consultant's job is to question the question, or reframe the problem. And so that's what I did. I asked Julie about her business and the different types of jewellery she made. I also asked her about her existing customers, sales patterns, pricing, distribution methods, and other aspects of her enterprise.

Julie's business was relatively simple. She designed and manufactured fine silver jewellery, and she also made brightly coloured acrylic jewellery. She loved both products equally and both were products of her creativity, skill and labour. In telling me about her customers they fell broadly into two camps: wealthy middle-aged ladies and teenage girls. Obviously, the customers for fine silver jewellery were wealthy middle-aged ladies, and she sold brightly coloured acrylic jewellery to teenage girls.

In many ways she had two businesses. Looking at her business from her own point of view, from the inside, it was one integrated business. She had one workshop, one business name, and one bank account. However, looking at her business from the customers' point of view, it was two different businesses. This is a crucial distinction to make.

I worked with Julie using the 3Ms technique...

Firstly we looked at the fine silver jewellery. What was the market? Clearly it is wealthy middle-aged ladies. Secondly, I asked about the message we want to convey to this audience about this product. By tightly controlling the questions in this way, we generated good answers – 'elegant', 'exclusive', 'handmade', 'expensive', 'classic' – appropriate keywords to craft our message around. These words were at the heart of what we wanted to say. Thirdly, we considered the medium. What was the most appropriate medium to deliver our message of elegance to those particular customers?

To decide this, we have to understand the customer – we have to look at the world from their point of view. What are their habits? How do they behave? What are their preferences? Who are their friends? Who has their trust? Whom do they believe? Let's go and ask them... As a result, we came to the conclusion that perhaps the most appropriate medium to convey this message is a feature or advertisement in one of the glossy lifestyle magazines that these ladies are known to read. These magazines fit with their own image and preferences. And so, having considered this product, identified its markets, and crafted a message, we concluded that the best medium to convey the message is an advert or editorial feature in one of these magazines.

Then we moved on to the second product, brightly coloured acrylic jewellery. Again, using the 3Ms, we asked firstly about the target market for these bangles and necklaces, and we know that the customers are teenage girls. Next we moved on to the message. I asked about the keywords we'd use to communicate our product to teenage girls. 'Fun', 'inexpensive', 'colourful' and 'cool', are the words that this question provoked. Finally we come to the third M, the medium. What's the most appropriate medium to convey this message to teenage girls? We're forced to imagine how teenage girls behave, their lifestyles, and the media they use and trust. Framing the question in this way, we conclude that social media such as Facebook, Twitter and text messages are the most appropriate media to use.

This is a simple example of the effectiveness of the '3Ms of marketing' technique. **Market**, **Message** and **Medium** – crucially, in that order. By considering each of the 3Ms in the right order, we're guided into making the right decisions about marketing communications.

Firstly, select the target markets. Or more precisely, the different target markets that apply to any one particular product or service. So for each product, we might list four or five targeted market segments.

Secondly, for each market segment, decide on the marketing message. (At this stage, just the heart of the message, keywords etc. Precise copywriting can be done later.) Note that it's possible – and indeed probable – that even for the same product we need different messages for different market segments. For example, some people will buy a product because of its comfort and another type of customer might buy the very same product because of its style.

Finally, we need to consider the most appropriate medium, or media, to convey each message to its target audience. Again, depending on the audiences we're targeting, we might choose different media to deliver the same message (or a different one) to different types of customer.

This methodology ensures that we design clear and precise communications with each target audience, for each product or service. In writing a marketing communications plan using the 3Ms, we end up with a plan based on precise 'straight lines', rather than a tangle of different messages being fired in all directions towards difference types of customer.

I use this methodology in my training workshops and in my consultancy work with clients. First of all I use case studies and examples from other kinds of businesses in order to illustrate how the technique works.

One of the reasons that the 3Ms technique works so well is that it forces us to consider the medium to be used in conveying marketing communications, only **after** we've decided on the target audience and the message. Without using 3Ms, what often happens is that the medium is decided too early in the process. It may be, for example, that there's an enthusiasm to use social media, or a special offer at the local print shop tempts us to produce leaflets, or we select a radio advertisement because we were impressed by how effective this medium was for another business.

This is how marketing communications often go wrong. Leaflets are produced without being clear where we'll distribute them – the distribution question comes last because it is the last element of the physical process of design-print-distribution. In fact, the process should start with the audience and, consequently, we should know who we're addressing from the very beginning. We then work 'backwards' to deciding the message for that particular audience and, **lastly,** decide on the vehicle to convey that message to those people. By doing it this way we come to much more useful conclusions about the medium to be employed.

'Easy! Obvious! It's just common sense!'

That's what my workshop participants say. My retort is that their new conclusions are totally different than their initial answers. I remind them that earlier they were saying why a colour brochure might be the best thing to do, or advocating a better website as a preferable medium.

It's only because they were guided by the 3Ms technique, one question at a time, in a logical order, that they came to conclusions arising from the 3Ms that make perfect sense. Without the 3Ms they were being imprecise, discussing the merits of various media in general, without considering them in the context of Julie's particular business, her products, and her target markets.

If we are to use our resources cost-effectively – if we're to be clear to ourselves and to our customers, and if we want to increase sales and profits – then we need to be precise about our marketing communications. The 3Ms of marketing technique is a simple but highly effective methodology to help us achieve that precision.

Key Points

The 3Ms technique forces us to think through marketing communications in the right order: Market, then Message, and then Medium.

What to do next

- Use the 3Ms technique to review your own marketing communications.

See also...

58 To tweet or not to tweet, that is the question

'You should use Twitter more,' said Patrick, a social media consultant I was chatting to at a networking event for creative and digital businesses. He told me about several of his clients who'd increased sales through effective use of Facebook, Twitter and other social media channels. In his enthusiasm he was encouraging everyone to join the party and benefit from the new social media revolution. The only trouble was that Patrick hadn't first asked me what my business objectives were, who were my target customers, and what were the messages I want to convey to them. In my view, the benefits of any particular medium can only be evaluated in relation to target markets and the particular messages to be communicated with them. Twitter might or might not be the best medium to use in any particular circumstance. Anyone who tries to sell you a medium without first asking about your markets and messages isn't worth listening to. Even if the medium they are selling is a 'sexy' one. I switched off and politely moved on.

Working with media businesses, I often hear discussions about the merits of certain media for marketing communications. It may be enthusiasm about online video, blogs, social media, TV advertising or eBooks. These discussions are meaningless outside the context of a particular business, its products, and its markets. Only then can we assess the pros and cons of any particular medium. It all depends on how appropriate they are in conveying a particular message to a particular audience.

We can only ever have a meaningful conversation about the pros and cons of any particular medium if we have a clear marketing strategy.

Key Points

The pros and cons of any medium can only be evaluated in the context of the business objectives, prioritisation of markets and key messages.

What to do next

- Challenge anyone advising you about marketing media. Insist that they first summarise your business objectives, chosen markets and key messages. Only then can they explain logically why a particular medium is the most appropriate.

See also...

59 How to be a great salesperson

Once I accompanied a friend to buy a car. She'd moved house and, as a result, had enough cash to buy a car outright. She didn't need a loan and was hoping for a substantial discount for a cash payment. We arrived at the car showroom and were greeted by a young salesman who immediately started his patter... He talked about how the company was offering 0% finance on loans for cars purchased before the end of the month, and spoke with enthusiasm about the attractive terms they could offer, how quickly the paperwork could be done, and the repayment period. When he eventually paused for breath, my friend simply turned and walked away.

She had no interest whatsoever in credit terms. She was offended that the salesman hadn't offered the simple courtesy of asking her what she wanted. Not only is it discourteous, it's very bad business. The salesman had no real interest in what the customer wanted. He was more obsessed about winning his commission from signing up another customer to 0% finance, whether or not they wanted it. If only that salesmen had listened for a moment. He would have changed his sales pitch entirely. He could have saved his own time and that of the customer by not talking about 0% finance. Instead he could have offered a cash discount. He might have sold a car.

The stereotype of a salesperson is a sleek-suited, fast-talking, hard-hitting, high-pressure salesman who has the 'gift of the gab'. He talks **at** customers until they buy what they're supposed to buy. In fact, contrary to this stereotype, the best salespeople listen first. Because by listening, they understand what the customer actually wants. Then when they speak they offer something that fits the needs and wants of the customer.

Another example is from my own experience. I was invited to a lunch meeting with a potential client, Simon. I had heard that his business development agency had an interest in sponsoring a reprint of one of my books. I was excited about this prospect – in my briefcase I had copies of the book and some notes about how we might achieve a deal. I had prepared in my mind how I would express the benefits to their organisation of reprinting my book, and was ready in my own particular way to make a sales pitch.

We started the lunch meeting with small talk about his work. I asked about his current projects and the challenges ahead. Eager though I was to get on with the business of selling my book, for some reason I took a more relaxed attitude and asked more questions. In response, Simon said that they had recently decided that their promotional material should be less paper-based and much more focused on digital media and online distribution. He also told me that they had commissioned a new website, which would be hungry for content. At this point I decided to change tack entirely. I left my book in my briefcase and abandoned the sales pitch I'd rehearsed in my head. After listening to what he had to say, I realised that a printed book wouldn't suit their requirements. Instead they needed something much more in fitting with their new digital strategy. I suggested that I produce some articles and short videos based on interviews with entrepreneurs, to publish on the new website. This was much more appropriate and achieved a positive response. I was awarded a contract.

I remember this because it worked so well – and because it was such an exception to my normal way of selling. I was about to fall into the trap that so many of us fall into. We talk rather than listen. It's so easy to do, mainly because we're so enthusiastic about our product. And of course because we want to make a sale. It can also be because we're nervous, and sometimes anxiety expresses itself through talking. Listening is more difficult – it requires restraint based on confidence and non-desperation. Ironically, when we're desperate, we tend to talk too much and have less chance of achieving a sale. Whereas when we're speaking from a position of comfort, without being desperate for the sale, there's more chance that we will be relaxed and listen. This puts us into a stronger position to respond appropriately with the right kind of product or service. As a result, a sale is more likely.

Key Points

Listening is a key part of selling. By listening you can address the customer's needs and wants more precisely.

What to do next

- Be prepared to listen. Listen to potential customers before making your sales pitch. And don't forget to listen to current customers about their next requirements.

- Make it a habit to listen before selling. Make a note of the occasions on which you do this.

See also...

60 You're the best salesperson

Often a creative entrepreneur will tell me that they're considering hiring a salesperson in order to win new business. They've found the budget to employ a 'business development manager' on a high salary, plus commission. They need more contracts but don't have time to go out themselves and call on potential new clients.

I am often sceptical of this approach.

In businesses where there needs to be a trusted relationship between supplier and client, a new salesperson is rarely in a position to win the necessary trust. Yes, they can convey to target clients the company's competences, what it can do, at what price, and even how it will do it. However this approach is often ineffective because the salesperson doing the talking is not actually the person with whom they will actually be working. The salesperson is not the one they need to trust. The people they **do** need to trust are the people who stay back in the office, who don't want to meet new clients. They tell me they don't have the time to win new business. Yet the most important link between the customer and the company is with the managing director and core staff.

The best person to sell the business to new clients is the boss.

Not only can they talk best about the company's competences, but they personify the company and its human bond with the client. In short, the client needs to be able to look someone in the eyes and decide whether this person really understands their needs and will actually deliver. That person is not the salesman but the boss. They are the person responsible for the company's reputation, its delivery on time and on budget, and the person who personifies the ethos of the business.

This tendency towards hiring a salesperson ties in with the mistaken belief that marketing is actually about the glamorous process of winning new customers. In reality, some of the most effective marketing is about retaining existing customers, winning repeat business, and increasing the lifetime value of current clients.

It's actually easier and therefore more cost-effective than winning new customers. Who is the person who is best placed to do this? The boss. The person that the client has come to know, to trust, has seen deliver, and likes to work with. Therefore, sometimes I have found myself advising the company not to employ a new business development manager. Instead, they should use the resources to buy time for the managing director to visit existing and past clients and take them for lunch. Over lunch they could find out about their current and impending needs, remind them of the excellent work they've done, and encourage them to recommend the company to other potential clients through good old word-of-mouth.

The chief executive is also the chief marketing officer. Not only are they responsible for strategic marketing, they might also be the best salesperson in the company.

Key Points

Consider carefully the pros and cons of employing a salesperson. It may be that the most effective salesperson is actually the chief executive. This is especially the case when approaching existing and past customers for more business.

What to do next

- Review your marketing strategy. Is it focused on winning totally new customers or does it involve getting more business from past and current customers?

- Ask the chief executive (who may be you) to spend 10% of their time winning more business from existing and past customers they know.

See also...

61 Customers are 'ploggers'

Customers are powerful.

We can't control customers and we can't control what they say.
All we can do is guide them to some extent. We can provide them
with the stories they will tell.

It's interesting to look at the progress of this thing called 'marketing'.
Around 50 years ago, marketing communications was all about
one-way advertising. It was a monologue. It was big companies
broadcasting their message through a limited number of media
outlets to a passive audience. First on the radio, then later on
TV, advertisements were one-to-many communications and the
advertiser controlled the message. Of course there was word-of-
mouth between individual customers on the ground, but they didn't
have the same power as advertisers to speak to masses of people.
Advertisers were firmly in control.

As companies began to realise that customers might have
something useful to say, marketing became a dialogue. This became
a two-way process, not equally two ways, but communication
from customer to company became increasingly important within
the wider marketing process. Nowadays this has developed even
further, and customers are even more powerful. In the 21st century
customers have access to the internet. They can communicate
not only with their immediate neighbours, but with communities
worldwide; an online campaign can counter a corporation's
message or destroy its reputation; a blogger can bring down
a company.

Word-of-mouth is now electronic, rapid and global. We've moved
from monologue, to dialogue, to 'poly-logue'. 'Polylogue' is a word
I have coined meaning 'many people talking amongst themselves'.
Yes, the customers are the poly-loguers, or let's say 'ploggers'.
No matter what your advertising message, the reality is that
customers will do the plogging. Be aware of this. Perhaps all we can
do, when faced with this power of customers, is be authentic and be
honest. The truth will out.

Customers want a story. 'Buzz marketing' is about the way a story spreads about a product or service or brand. People tell stories and the currency of conversation is tales, not advertising slogans. Perhaps all we can do is give them a tale to tell. Give them the true story of our brand. Tell them what we did, including what we did wrong and how we put it right. Tell them where we're coming from. Tell them about ourselves and our people. Be open about our passions and beliefs. They will find out anyway, soon enough, so why not tell them now?

Recognise the power of customers and provide stories for their plogging.

Key Points

Customers talk with each other like never before. Word of mouth is electronic, rapid and global. Advertisers no longer control the message; customers do. All we can do is be open and give them stories to tell.

What to do next

- Tell customers about your company, your values, and your ambitions. And then remain true to them. Good stories about your business will spread. But beware, because bad stories will spread further.

- Add a section to your website (and other marketing communications) about your own and your company's back story, its values and its ambitions.

See also...

62 Why advertising can lose you money

A young entrepreneur was telling me that a recent advertising campaign had been successful because it had more than paid for itself in increased sales for his photography business. Kevin told me that he'd spent $10,000 on advertising but the campaign had brought in extra sales of $12,000 for his photographic art prints. Kevin was pleased with his success.

I was concerned about his calculations and doubted whether the campaign had actually been profitable at all. We have to remember that the cost of advertising and other promotional activity needs to be exceeded not by additional **revenue** generated, but by additional **profits** generated.

I asked about the profitability of his $12,000 sales and discovered that the cost of sales had been over $3,000. This included the cost of producing the prints and the associated packing and postage costs. Even without taking into account other costs and business overheads, his profit on these sales was less than $9,000. He'd spent $10,000 to make $9,000.

Sadly, Kevin isn't unique in making the mistake of comparing advertising costs with sales rather than profit. In order to make rational decisions about how much extra revenue needs to be achieved by any advertising investment, entrepreneurs need to have accurate financial information available about the full costs associated with each of their products, services or projects. This means understanding our business finances in more detail and doing the sums properly.

Key Points

Don't make the mistake of justifying advertising spend by measuring increased sales. Advertising investment needs to be exceeded by additional **profits** generated.

What to do next

- Fully analyse the costs associated with each product, service or project in your enterprise in order to be able to calculate profitability. This information can then be used to evaluate more precisely the cost effectiveness of any advertising campaign.

See also...

63 Marketing is the chief executive's responsibility

Marketing is **not** about sprinkling some kind of magic dust to make any product or service sell. Marketing is **not** the job of the sales department. Strategic marketing is the responsibility of the chief executive, who must make sure that the business is viable and continues to be so, by aligning the company's products to the changing needs of its selected customers.

Marketing is actually a perspective on the whole business: it's the top-level strategy that decides what to produce and which markets to target. When this fundamental responsibility is ignored by top management, in the false belief that marketing is simply about promotion and sales, the business fails.

These fundamental marketing decisions are difficult to make, because they're not about the extras, the frills, the add-ons, but are actually at the very heart of the business. Someone has to decide whether or not the business's products and services are good enough for the target market, with whom to compete (and not compete) in the marketplace, and which market sectors should be targeted (and which ones not targeted).

This requires a lot of thought, good judgement, research and information, and tough decisions.

That's why many people get marketing wrong – because it's difficult. It's much, much easier to ignore the fundamental problems and instead hire more salespeople, or put pressure on the sales department, or invest in a new promotional campaign.

But that is to shirk responsibility and avoid the big important issues. Somebody needs to devise a realistic and effective marketing strategy. That's the job of the chief executive.

Key Points

Strategic marketing is a top-level responsibility and so the chief executive is the chief marketing officer. It's not easy but it's got to be done. That's what chief executives are paid for.

What to do next

- Check to what extent the chief executive (that might be you) is taking responsibility for devising and implementing an effective and realistic marketing strategy.

- Write down your marketing strategy and share a summary of this with everyone in the enterprise.

See also...

Thinking clearly about different markets helps us to be strategic about marketing.

Simple but effective tools like the '3Ms of Marketing' help us to be precise.

Link this precision with authenticity by regarding yourself and others at the heart of your business as the main sales people.

This powerful combination of precision and authenticity is what marketing is really about.

Perhaps now is the time to go back to the beginning of the book and remember Nick's authentic marketing...

We need both strategy and communications

In marketing, we need both strategy and communications. A sound strategy that can't be translated into effective communications will not achieve its objectives. Equally, clever communications that are not strategically focused might entertain consumers but will not deliver sales.

Brilliant communication will not make up for a lack of a sound strategy based on a clear understanding of our objectives, competitiveness and target markets.

It's vital that any marketing communications are undertaken only after having devised an effective strategy. This strategy provides a framework for communications to selected markets, with focused messages, delivered using the most appropriate media.

Marketing in its fullest sense is complex and embraces a whole range of activities connecting fundamental business strategy at its core with effective communications. It must involve everyone within a business for this to work properly. It involves both left-brain thinking and right-brain thinking. It needs to take place in the boardroom first. It must engage people working in both the studio and the business office.

Marketing is both hard work and fun. It can be both logical and quirky. It's creative in both senses of the word. It uses both a-Creativity and i-Creativity; artistic creativity and a broader ingenuity. It's a comprehensive process of running our businesses based on an analytic understanding of our competitive advantage, the careful selection of the most appropriate customers, and activities that fit with our values. This will deliver success in the terms we have defined for ourselves.

If we get the marketing strategy right first, the marketing communications are much more likely to be effective. In fact, if we get our marketing strategy right, marketing communications are relatively easy and we don't need to do the 'hard sell'.

The most difficult part is thinking through the strategy. Yes, thinking is the real hard work. Don't avoid this and go for the lazy option of working hard being active. Don't be a busy fool.

Work hard to get the marketing strategy right and then all the rest of it is the easy stuff, mere detail.

Think smart. Be rational – and then, if need be, be quirky.

What to do next

You've reached the end of the book but improvements in marketing know no end. We can always improve our endeavours. And in any case, we live in a fast-changing world: customers' needs change over time; new competitors emerge; the world changes around us. We can never be complacent.

So this isn't really the end. It's certainly not the end of applying strategic marketing principles to our businesses. It's not even the end of the book, because it's been designed for you to read in a non-linear way. Dip into it daily to provoke new ideas and discover insights for your enterprise. Use the tips and techniques. Follow the links to associated sections and external links.

Let me know how strategic marketing helps your own business to become even more successful. I'm always on the lookout for success stories and examples of smart marketing to write about. Email me at david@davidparrish.com. If I write about your experiences in later editions of this book or other writings, I'll acknowledge your business and provide a link if possible.

Tell your colleagues, contacts and friends about this book.

Please write a review of this book. To read some reviews and for links to book review pages on eBook platforms, go to the Chase One Rabbit[16] page on my website.

Read my other book 'T-Shirts and Suits: A Guide to the Business of Creativity' in paperback[17] or as a free eBook[18].

---

16 www.chaseonerabbit.com

17 www.tss-book.com

18 www.tss-ebook.com

Share your marketing successes and learn from other entrepreneurs on the T-Shirts and Suits Creative Enterprise Network[19] and the groups on Facebook[20], Linked In[21] and Google+[22].

Download and share the free business development resources available on my website[23].

For more information about my consultancy, training and public speaking work internationally, see www.davidparrish.com.

I wish you every success in using strategic marketing profitably in your own business.

---

19 www.tss-cen.com

20 www.facebook.com/groups/2404983690/

21 www.linkedin.com/groups?gid=1944668

22 https://plus.google.com/114412479781472674998/about

23 www.tss-freestuff.com

Acknowledgements

I would like to thank everyone who has helped me to write this book.

Fiona Shaw was my editor, manager and coach on the journey from this book being just an idea to a finished product. The book would not exist without her professional help and friendly support. Thanks Fiona.

Several people generously agreed to read drafts of the book and offer their feedback, and many colleagues and friends helped in other ways, including:

Shelley Jayne Crawford, Jonathan Gibaud, Rob Kinsey, Christopher Moss, Alun Parry, Jan Peters, Cathy Skelly, Gary Smailes, Judith Mansell, Mark McGuinness, Kevin McManus, John Meadowcroft, Kath Oversby, Adriana Ursache, Elisabeth Vaneveld.

In addition I would like to thank the thousands of creative entrepreneurs from around the world whom I have had the privilege to meet, as a business adviser, trainer and speaker. I'm constantly learning from them and drawing inspiration from the way they combine their creativity with smart business thinking. There are too many to name, but thanks to all of you.

As well as the people leading and managing design, media and technology businesses in the creative, cultural and digital industries worldwide, I would like to thank the specialist development agencies that support them, with whom I often work in partnership. Amongst all these, a special mention must go to Merseyside ACME at Liverpool Vision in England.